KLONDIKE
HOUSE

Memories of an Irish Country Childhood

John Dwyer

DEDICATION

To my daughter Grace, with all my love.

CONTENTS

ACKNOWLEDGMENTS

There are many people I'd like to thank for their help in getting this book ready for publication:

Sarah Lovell for her excellent edits. She never refused a request to look over a chapter and I thank her for that.
Steve Warner for casting his eyes over every chapter and offering his insightful advice.
My Mum for her advice on the final draft.
Patrick Sullivan, on who's research much of the story "Klondike House" is based. Also for his permission to reproduce his photograph of Mike Dwyer.
Michael Ome Untiedt for his kind permission to reproduce his fantastic painting for my book cover.
My uncle Michael Dwyer for his permission to reproduce his poem.
Dominic Taylor, Ger Harrington, Kieran Harrington, Noel Phylan for their help with reviews and feedback.
My former teacher Mrs. Power for helping to jog my memory about my days at Kilmacowen school.
Finally, thanks to my wonderful wife Caroline for her endless support and welcome cups of hot tea – both essential while I was working on getting this book finished on time.

1 SCHOOL DAYS AT KILMACOWEN

The smell is what I remember most about my first day at school. It took me a while to notice it, as I was so engrossed with my new surroundings. It wasn't even my first full day, just a short visit to Kilmacowen School to show me where I'd be going the following term. While my mother talked with the teacher in the hall, I wandered happily around the classroom. The voices of excited pupils echoed around the sparse room as they made the most of their teacher's absence. The older ones craved mischief and saw me as a perfect opportunity to do just that. One of them coaxed me to his desk and told me to tell the teacher that she had a big head. Thankfully, I was so absorbed with my new world that I forgot to inform her about her cranial problem. I gawked up at the lofty ceilings of peeling paint, the old floorboards creaking with each step I took. A worn fireguard stood before the unlit fireplace. A huge map of the world hung beside a bookcase of disorganised files and folders. Fresh air billowed through the open windows and offered a respite from the heat of the day. Despite that, there was a strange odour in the classroom. It was vaguely familiar to me, even as a five-year-old boy. It reminded me of a time my father brought me setting traps for rabbits. He checked any burrows we found to see if they were occupied, as many rabbit holes had been abandoned. The holes that housed rabbits had a peculiar smell from them, an earthy musk that was part damp, part rot. That smell is what I remember most about Kilmacowen National School in 1977.

At the start of the following school term in September, it was time for me to return to Kilmacowen on a full-time basis. On my first morning, I walked with my mother to the bottom of our laneway, holding her hand and excitedly asking her a deluge of questions about the day ahead. My new schoolbag bulged with fresh copybooks, pencils, crayons, sandwiches, a bottle of milk and an apple. We waited by the road until Brendan Sullivan came along. He was our neighbour's son and had attended Kilmacowen School for the previous two years. He had been asked to accompany me on the road for the first few weeks until I could manage safely on my own.

"Take care now Johnny and be good for your teacher," my mother said before kissing me on the head.

I joined Brendan and waved goodbye to my mother to start my new life as a full-time pupil. It was a great adventure to be going away for the day with Brendan and I didn't feel the slightest bit lonely for my parents. The school was over two miles away from our house and it took at least forty minutes to get there. We walked along the quiet Lack Road until it joined the main road to Castletownbere at the Fiddler's Cross. There was no footpath on the main road so we had to keep into the ditch when we heard a car coming. Once we passed the green letterbox, we turned left onto the Kilmacowen road. Most children walked to school when the days were dry and cars were rare enough on the road. I heard the din of children playing in the yard well before the school itself came into view.

The plaque on the wall of the school declared that it had opened in 1870. It was a sturdy, slate-roofed building, dwarfed by the impressive bulk of Maulin Mountain to the east. Some pine trees grew inside the school wall and a stream flowed by the western gable before joining the Kealincha River. The small cluster of houses that made up Kilmacowen lay just up the road and a patchwork of rough fields surrounded the school. The homes that dotted the surrounding countryside provided the children that attended the school.

We were slightly early so we waited in the yard with the other children. The teacher arrived soon after and opened the school door. The school's only teacher was Mrs. Power, a kind and patient woman who had the job of teaching six classes of twenty-one children. Thinking that school was an extension of home, I asked her to take off my jacket and hang it up for me, much to her amusement. With a gentle smile, she encouraged me to learn to do it myself. Once that was sorted, she welcomed me to the school and showed me to my seat. It was an old wooden unit with the desk joined to the bench. The top of the desk opened to reveal a compartment for holding books and pencils. The cast-iron supports felt cold against my legs as I eased myself into the seat. There was even a disused inkwell on the top of the desk, splattered with ancient stains. The desk's surface was as smooth as wax from the generations of arms that had rubbed against it. It was heavily tattooed with the names of past pupils, many of whom were dead at that stage. It was so crowded with names that many had written theirs on top of others. My desk was a memorial to all those who had come and gone from the school.

Kilmacowen School, now a renovated private residence

I quickly adapted to my new environment and the weeks flew by. Every morning, Mrs. Power took a roll call. When she called my name in Gaelic, I answered "anseo", which meant, "present". She wrote the record of attendance into a long and ancient-looking tome with tattered edges. Once roll call finished, Mrs. Power started class for the day. She wrote our lessons on an old blackboard, using each side for different classes. She was kept busy as she switched from teaching one class to another in an instant.

At lunchtime, we ate in a disused room next to the main classroom. They were both the same size but instead of desks, it had long wooden benches placed against the walls. I opened my bag to see what my mother had made for me. Lunch was usually two sandwiches of homemade bread and butter, filled with blackberry jam, ham or cheese. I washed down my food with a bottle of milk. In the winter months, the milk felt icy cold going down my throat but, in the summer, the heat sometimes turned it sour by lunchtime. When it was too wet to play outside, we played in the same room. The racket of laughing children echoing around the sparse room was deafening.

Thankfully, most days we played in the schoolyard. The yard was a narrow strip of stony ground at the back of the school, bounded by a high earthen fence. We played football there and raced each other up and down the yard. We had to be careful not to kick the ball onto the road, as Mrs. Power would confiscate it for our own safety. The road was a dangerous place for children to be chasing a ball. After a wayward kick, a chorus of groans followed the ball as it disappeared with Mrs. Power through the school door. Being one of the oldest children, we begged Paul Hanley to go into the school and get the ball back for us. Sometimes he emerged empty handed, shrugging his shoulders. Most times, however, he emerged with a wide grin as he held the precious ball aloft, like the captain of a winning football team displaying the trophy. We poured congratulations on him before starting the game again. As Mrs. Power told me since, we became very good at keeping the ball in the yard.

When we weren't playing football, we raced each other. Paul Hanley picked teams of runners for relay races. The competitors sprinted up and down the yard, passing a stick to the next teammate who scampered off in the opposite direction. When my turn came and a breathless sprinter passed me the stick, I took off as fast as I could towards the end of the yard. Unfortunately, I was running against a girl blessed with an enormous stride and she glided past me with ease as I struggled to keep up with her. I mustn't have made much of an impression as a relay runner as I wasn't asked to run after that. Instead, I joined the other non-Olympians up on the grassy-topped ditch that surrounded the school and played cowboys and Indians. I found I was much better at playing dead.

Since the school had no electricity, class finished at three in the afternoon to avoid the evening darkness. My grandparents lived a hundred yards from the Fiddler's Cross so I often visited them before going home. In truth, the visit was more in hope of a bowl of my grandmother's rice pudding with brown sugar. She sometimes gave me a Catholic magazine called "The Messenger" to give to Peg Donovan as I was passing her house on my way home. She also gave me letters to post to her family in America when I passed the letterbox in the morning. When they were ripe, I feasted on blackberries from the briars when they were out in late September. Over the previous months, I watched them change from white flowers, to hard red berries and finally, to luscious black delights. I lost track of time as I skipped from bush to bush, picking off the soft fruit. When I got home, my blackened mouth betrayed the reason I was so late getting home.

With the arrival of autumn, the days shortened and the mornings became much colder. The classroom always seemed to be in near darkness as the only illumination came through the windows. The open fireplace provided the only source of heat in the school. Each morning we needed a fire, Mrs. Power told the older boys to cross into the neighbouring fields in search of brisna, small twigs used to start the fire. They were delighted to be asked, as it was a chance to be out of class. They made sure they took their time gathering the brisna. I longed to join them and often asked to do so but I was too young. Once the boys returned, Mrs. Power used the brisna they had gathered to start the fire. Soon after, she brought in coal from the outside shed and poured in onto the flames. Only when the fire was blazing could class begin. On numerous mornings, it was so wet outside that the brisna couldn't be collected, so we went through the day without heat.

The school toilet was an outhouse in every sense of the word. It was a small building, separate from the school and backed onto the nearby stream. A wall separated the boys and girls toilets but they were in the same building. Inside, was a raised wooden bench with a large hole cut in it to sit on. There was no flushing system and human waste simply fell into the nearby stream. The smell of the place during the hot summer months was unforgettable.

Once we were finished, we walked down to the same stream to wash our hands, making very sure we were upstream from the toilets. The school had no running water, even for drinking. Mrs. Power again sent some older children to the stream to fill bottles. They were then placed near the fireplace to be used as drinking water.

My only classmate was Pat Sheehan, a local boy from Kilmacowen. We were the only two children to enrol at Kilmacowen School that year. Since there were only two of us in the youngest class, we played with toy blocks while Mrs. Power spent time with the other classes. While playing one day, a small toy block fell into a hole in the floorboards near my desk and I dipped my hand in to retrieve it. Mrs. Power spotted me and shrieked, "John, take your hand out of there at once!" I whipped my hand back quickly and looked at her with a puzzled expression. What had I done wrong? She immediately led me out of the classroom and took me to the nearby stream. There, she washed my hands in the icy water with a bar of strong smelling Life Buoy soap.

"Don't ever put your hands in there again," she scolded me gently.

A few days later, a man came into the classroom with a bucket in his hand. He nodded to Mrs. Power before heading over towards my desk and kneeling down on the floorboards. He scooped some stuff from the bucket with a small spade and dropped it into the hole where my block had fallen. When I got home that evening, I told my mother about the strange visitor. She told me the old school had rats and that the man was putting down poison for them. That explained the strange smell that hung around the school. It was from the rats that lived and died under the very floorboards we walked on.

One morning, while waiting for Mrs. Power to arrive at school, some joker decided to add a little excitement to the day by inserting small stones in the keyhole of the school door. When Mrs. Power arrived and tried to open it, the key wouldn't work. She tried it a number of times but to no avail. At that stage, we gathered around her, trying to see what was happening. I entertained exciting images of her shrugging her shoulders and telling us to go home for the day, as she couldn't open the door. Unfortunately, Mrs. Power eventually saw the stones in the keyhole and asked for a knitting needle from one of the girls. She carefully forced the stones out with the needle and opened the door, to a chorus of groans. Yet another reason to hate knitting, I thought.

Last pupils to attend Kilmacowen School. The author is pictured standing in the middle of the front row.

The school had been built during a time when the local population demanded it, but now, there were only twenty-one pupils enrolled. In addition, the poor state of the building meant it was unsuitable for education. A new school had been built near the village of Eyeries and we were due to move there at the start of the following school year.

On our last day at Kilmacowen School before it closed, Mrs. Power looked around at the walls of peeling paint, her arms folded across her chest. She seemed to be taking the place in for the last time. She was the last in a long line of teachers that stretched back over a hundred years. There was emotion in her voice as she wished us all a happy summer and hoped to see us in the new school in September. She dismissed us for the last time and we poured through the door to the waiting summer. Mrs. Power locked the old door, leaving the old building to the rats. Nobody was going to care about the smell anymore.

2 A TALE OF TWO BRIDGES

"The bridge is gone," my father announced solemnly one morning as I ate breakfast with my brothers and sisters. Water dripped from his raincoat, forming a growing puddle around his boots. Our chatter ceased at the news and we looked at each other in astonishment. After quickly finishing our food, we pulled on our coats and went to see for ourselves. The bridge was near my grandparent's house and it took us fifteen minutes to get there on foot. By then, the worst of the previous night's torrential rain had eased, but the pitter-patter of drops still rattled on my hood as I ran down the lane towards the river. The roar of the floodwaters grew as we neared the bridge. When I saw the destruction, I just stood and gaped. The old bridge was broken in two, its main walkway submerged under fast-flowing waves of earthy water. I was shaken at the sight, as I imagined the bridge would last forever. My father joined us, as we stood transfixed by the scene.

"A new bridge will have to be built," he said in a hushed tone, almost to himself. Without saying another word, he returned to the house, leaving us mesmerised by the floods tumbling over the broken bridge. I thought if anyone could build a bridge across the Kealincha River, it would be my father.

* * *

The Kealincha River, which destroyed the bridge that night, ran directly through our land. I was proud of the fact that it was the longest river in the Beara Peninsula. It was still some way short of great rivers such as the Nile and the Amazon but, for this rugged peninsula in the southwestern corner of Ireland, it was good enough. It had its source high up in Maulin, an Ayer's Rock of a mountain that dominated the horizon to the east of our farm. Maulin had a deep cleft gouged on one side that I fancied had been made by a meteor thousands of years ago. Numerous streams fed the young river as it dashed past the townland of Kilmacowen before slowing through the fertile Inches Valley. Further downstream, it formed an impressive cascade as the water tumbled across rocks and boulders above the ruins of an old mill. The river finally reached its end at Eyeries Strand where it emptied into the Atlantic waters of Coulagh Bay. We farmed on the banks of that river as it flowed through the Inches Valley, as had my grandfather and his father.

Like most farms in Beara, it was small but enough to rear some cattle and sheep, as well as to grow vegetables. Despite the beauty of the whole river, the section that ran through our land was the dearest to me.

The beautiful cascades section of the Kealincha River

We were fortunate to have the river flow through our land, as we never had to be concerned about water for our cattle. However, it also split our farm in two and the old bridge had been the vital link between both swathes of land. Local farmers as well as hill-walkers and visitors used the bridge as a shortcut. Thousands of sheep and cattle traversed it going to and from our fields. It also kept lifelong friendships alive. My grandmother often asked me to accompany her across the bridge to visit her friend Mary, who lived in a whitewashed cottage on the other side. My Gran suffered from arthritis in her knees and needed me for support to cross the bridge. I remember how she squeezed my shoulder hard as she climbed the few steps to the bridge, her grasp only relaxing when she arrived safely on the other side.

The bridge also provided us with an ideal fishing hole. Here, the river tumbled into a deep pool strewn with rocks where fish were plentiful. After heavy rain, the water turned brown with earth and encouraged the fish to seek worms and, in turn, for us to seek them. On one such day, I accompanied my father to do some fishing. Before we left the house, he went to the old press in the kitchen and opened one of the drawers. He took out a spool of fishing line and a small tin box, which he put in his pocket before setting off for the river. I thought it was strange that he didn't take the homemade fishing pole that hung above the kitchen door but I didn't say anything.

When we got to the bridge, he set everything down on the bank and scanned the birch trees that grew near the river. He selected a long, slender branch from one of the trees and broke it off. He then took a penknife from his pocket and pruned the offshoots, creating a long, smooth pole. At one end, he cut a groove to secure the fishing line. He then took the tin box from his pocket and carefully selected a trout hook and a piece of lead. He secured the hook to the end of the line and tied the lead just above the hook. The lead was to keep the hook from floating to the surface, he explained. He then told me to get some worms for bait. Heaps of cow dung near our neighbour's shed yielded a rich supply of fat and lively worms for that purpose. I returned with a jar full of wriggly worms. My father picked one and impaled it on the hook. We were ready to start fishing.

I joined him on the riverbank just below the bridge and he showed me how to cast the line, to jerk it gently back and forth to attract the fish, and how to free a hook if it became ensnared in a hidden rock. He managed to catch two trout while he was showing me this. He then handed me the rod and let me do it myself, coaching me through the motions. A thrill of excitement ran through me when I got the first bite, that unmistakable tug at the end of the line. With my father's urgings, I pulled hard on the rod and at the end of the line was a trout. I landed him on the grassy bank where my father picked him up and showed me how to extract the hook before breaking its throat. I had caught my first fish and I was delighted with myself.

"That's your fishing rod now, look after it," my father said. It was the best present I could get.

A few weeks later, I was fishing with my new rod at that same spot when a man appeared on the opposite bank and started fishing. He wore a brown fishing jacket, a tweed hat, and adjusted a fine-looking reel at the end of his expensive fishing rod. He even used fly-hooks, something that I had never seen before. He fished in a manner that I had only seen on television before as he expertly whipped the fishing line in and out of the water with a flourish, looking every part the professional angler. We waved to each other and he tried to shout something to me but the roar of the tumbling waters drowned out his words. Instead, we returned to the pleasant business of fishing. I had a lucky day and, within half an hour of arriving, I caught three decent sized brown trout. Meanwhile, my friend across the river had nothing to show for his efforts but a frustrated look and fishing line that constantly tangled in a nearby bush. I impaled my catch with a sharpened stick, threw the homemade rod over my shoulder, and waved goodbye to my expert angler. He waved and was probably delighted to see the back of me. The trout ended up in the frying pan that evening along with some onions and wild mushrooms. There's something deeply satisfying about enjoying a meal that you caught yourself.

Along with providing food, the river also provided us with fun. Upstream from the old bridge, the fast-moving current had carved a deep pool in a bend and it proved to be an ideal spot for swimming. Deposits of sand and gravel below one bank made a basic but inviting beach. On a hot summer's day, the cool waters were heavenly, especially after working at the hay or the turf. I competed against my brothers and sisters to see who could hold their breath underwater the longest or make the biggest splash by jumping off the opposite bank. My brothers carted large stones and gravel to one end of the swimming hole in order to create a rough dam and raise the water level even more. After we had enough, we got out and lay on some towels. The sun-scorched stones on our beach felt like hot coals underfoot, making my toes curl. However, they felt lovely under a towel and I imagined that this was what life was like in places like Hawaii or California. On a good day, we might go swimming three or four times, eagerly looking forward to the next visit as soon as the previous one had finished.

On one occasion, we were enjoying the water when it suddenly turned murky brown. My brother Finbarr got out to investigate and returned shaking his head in dismay.

"The fecking cows are shitting in the river," he complained bitterly, pointing to the ford just upstream. We looked up to see the cattle standing in the water as they deposited manure in vast quantities. We begrudgingly abandoned our swim, sulking and cursing the cattle as we faced towards home with our clothes in hand. Blissfully unaware of having cut short our fun, the cows chewed the cud contentedly while continuing to decorate the water with dung.

During those idyllic summer months, the river gurgled softly like a baby on its way through our land. Swallows picked off insects as they swooped low above the tranquil water. Furze bushes blazed with yellow flowers and sweet honeysuckle scented the air. Primroses provided a guard of honour as the river meandered over lichen-covered rocks before forming wide glassy pools, green with slimy algae. The still surface was only broken by a jumping trout, which sent ripples radiating across the surface. In some years, when we had a particularly hot summer, the river would shrivel up to nothing more than a stream. On my way to the hill on one such day, I stopped at the river's edge to take a drink of water. As I did, a shrill cry pierced the silence. I was startled and nearly toppled into the river with fright. A magnificent Grey Heron spread its long wings and rose into the air like some prehistoric creature. I watched as it glided above the river, seeking out another spot to safely fish before disappearing in the distance.

Once those wonderful summer days started to shorten and fade, autumn and winter brought a change to the Kealincha River. Heavy rains thundered down from the heavens for days on end. Small streams that fed the river along its course turned into torrents and bulked the ever-growing body of water. By the time it passed through our land, the small river had become a roaring torrent of angry water. The gurgling baby of summer was now a wild animal that made me feel a little scared when I saw it up close. It was hard for me to imagine that much water coming down from the hills. Sometimes, I saw things carried along by the flood like a roll of sheep-wire, wooden fencing stakes or a small tree. I once saw a dead sheep carried along by the churning waters, its bloated body tumbling over repeatedly on its journey to the Atlantic Ocean. Large chunks of land, which river deposits had helped create over the centuries, were reclaimed within minutes by the powerful waters. Even stout and sturdy bridges would sometimes have to yield to such power.

Despite its robust construction, the river had been chipping away at the old bridge for decades. Like two ancient rivals, successive floods broke over the concrete structure and, each time, the waters subsided to reveal the bridge still standing. About ten years earlier, after some particularly severe flooding, the bridge showed its first signs of weakening. The raging waters had undermined the stout base, on which its survival depended. Large chunks of land around the bridge had also subsided, making it unstable. Despite the damage, the bridge was still safe to cross and served us for another few years. When she finally surrendered on that wet morning, it was the end of an era. I didn't realise it but, even as we watched the muddy waters coursing over her broken spine that morning, plans for a new bridge had already been set in motion. It was a big decision, as a previous project hadn't gone well.

Not long before, my father had tried to reclaim a weed-choked field across the river. This piece of ground was boggy and only fit for scrawny sheep. He refused to allow it go to waste so he set to work trying to reclaim it. My father first ploughed the ground and removed the roots of those wicked weeds. He then dug deep trenches along the field and filled them with stones to provide drainage. He finally replanted it with grass-seed and sprayed it with weed killer. Three months later, the previous waste ground was lush with green grass. We were delighted at this successful reclamation project and planned more. However, it wasn't to last. By the following year, those cruel weeds had returned stronger and more plentiful than ever. The sight of that field choked with weeds once more was a bitter pill to swallow. Great effort sometimes resulted in little or no reward in the life of a farmer. The sense of "why bother" seemed to prevail for a long time after that. The project of rebuilding a bridge across the river offered new hope to us.

A new bridge needed a new site, so my father chose a spot further upstream where the cows forded the river. Both he and my brother Finbarr worked many long, hard days there. The most important part of the job was getting the base right. If that wasn't strong enough, then the best bridge in the world wouldn't survive. I must admit, I often wondered at the wisdom of this endeavour. Building walls or a shed on dry land is one thing, but trying to put down a concrete foundation with water running around you is a different matter. In addition to that, they had the weather to contend with. During that year, heavy rains delayed the work by months. Only when the water level had fallen, could they both return to the painstaking task. Day after backbreaking day, they toiled at the bridge. One weekend, they managed to position the main concrete walkway across the river and the new bridge was finally taking shape. After a few more weeks, it was finished. Our land was once again connected. The bitter memory of the failed reclamation project was forgotten and a new spirit could be felt around the old place. A sturdy new bridge spanned the Kealincha once more and the grand old river had a new rival.

Relaxing at home that Christmas, I picked up a copy of the Eyeries Newsletter, an annual publication where people can submit details of all notable events that took place in the parish that particular year. I read the usual list of poems and stories submitted by locals when I came to a piece that caught my interest. As I read it, I realised that my father had written it. I was surprised as he is a modest man and doesn't tend to submit stories to any publications, even one as local as the Eyeries Newsletter. The story was about two bridges, one old and one new that both spanned the longest river in Beara.

The author's sister Marian standing on the new bridge across the Kealincha River.

After reading the piece, I understood the pride he felt in completing the new bridge and once again joining our land. He had not only built a bridge, he had built a monument, something solid and lasting. Maybe in time these words will become my own monument, my own bridge.

A Bridge Over Beara's Longest River
by John J. Dwyer

My memory now reminds me and takes me back to the summer of '45 when the Board of Works built a bridge across the river down behind our house. It served the people of this townland for 50 years, but then in 1995 it began to crumble due to heavy flooding during that span. We applied to several bodies for grant aid, and nothing happened. Then in December of '97, after heavy frost and a session of floods, it collapsed and fell in. It looked very much then like the end of an era for that old structure. Now how are we to get access to half our land, which lies at the south side of this river? I see only one way, and that would be to construct a new bridge further upstream, which I did during the summer of '98.

I first hired a JCB operator. Timmy Murphy was the man; he had foundations dug in a matter of minutes. Finbarr and myself poured concrete with the help of Patrick Lehane behind the mixer. We got up out of the riverbed in a very short time. It is now late May '98; the next subbie to arrive is Joe Sullivan "Gort" with his mobile welding apparatus. He bonded the big beams together forever. I applied the finishing touches myself. The job is now abandoned due to flooding.

It is now September '98, and I am awakened this Monday morning at 6 o' clock from torrential rainfall pounding the slate roof over my head. I get out and dress and look out the back window. I see floods everywhere. I get into my wellingtons and raincoat and go off down the laneway thinking of my unfinished work. When I approach the riverbank, all I can see of my bridge is the railing, but again my structure battled that mighty deluge.

It is 6.45 am, I am here watching this huge volume of water rushing down around the bends, and sailing on the surface of the current is a big tree, which was uprooted somewhere upriver; after that comes something like 3 or 4 stakes with a half coil of sheep wire attached, all en route for the blue horizon.

> *A winding river winds its way*
> *Close to my Irish home,*
> *As it finds its way into Coulagh Bay,*
> *Where it rolls the Atlantic foam.*

> *'Twas in a cot beside this spot*
> *Where the murmuring river flows,*
> *I waved my hand to the fields so grand,*
> *My lovely Irish home.*

Slán agaibh, agus Nollaig faoi shean agus faoi mhaise dhibh go leir.
[Goodbye to you all and have a happy and prosperous Christmas]

Seán O Duibhir
[John Dwyer]

3 A WOLF IN SHEEP'S CLOTHING

As The Beast charged at me, I remember thinking, "This can't be happening, sheep aren't meant to act like this." That was my last thought before a direct hit to the knees sent me cartwheeling through the air. Afterwards, even my father confessed that in all his years, he never came across such an aggressive and fearless animal. In the days after the attack, I tried to think of reasons why a sheep would act in such a, well, un-sheepish manner. I soon realised that they had good cause for complaint.

The morning of the attack was warm and mild when I departed for the hill with my father and two brothers. Our task that day was to gather our flock and bring them down to the shed near the house for dosing. We kept about three hundred Blackface sheep on the nearby hill during the mild summer months. Blackfaces were a hardy breed and perfectly suited to harsh conditions. The hill was commonage, so there was shared ownership between local farmers who had the right to graze it. There were no fences so the sheep could wander freely in search of forage. In winter, we brought them down from the barren hill to the fields around our house. Sheep farming was a full-time job and a tough one at that. In a hilly area like the Beara Peninsula, the job is even harder.

On our way up the hill road, we passed the Dipping Tank. This was a concrete enclosure where the local farmers brought their sheep to be dipped. Our neighbour Paddy O'Sullivan was dipping some sheep there with another man and my father stopped to ask if they'd seen any of our own on the hill. As my father spoke to Paddy, I watched the dipping process. The tank was a concrete well filled with water and mixed with sheep-dip, a pungent fluid designed to protect them against flies, ticks and lice. The sheep were forced along a narrow walkway before being pushed into the tank to join two or three others already thrashing about in there. It must have been a frightening experience for the sheep and, on a few occasions, some came close to drowning. After less than a minute, they each staggered up the ramp and out of the tank, coughing and spluttering.

Paddy had seen some of our sheep on the south side of the hill and we headed in that direction. When we got to the top of the hill road, my father told me to look for a sheep that had been missing for a few days.

"If you don't see the ewe with the others, you'll find her just below The Shelf," he advised me, referring to a cave in the hill. "That's where she usually stays at this time of day. You can't miss her, she has a speckled face," he said, with a wave of his hand to dismiss me. Too afraid to ask for more details, I trundled off in a state of despair — to me, all the sheep had speckled faces. Despite my apprehension, I couldn't help but marvel at how well he knew his flock. Even though over three hundred of them roamed the hill, he knew each sheep by their face, traits and movements.

Not long into my search, I came across the bloated remains of the speckled face ewe. Her back legs were sticking out from the hole of bog water into which she had fallen and drowned. Our blue identification mark was visible on her back. She wasn't the first sheep to have met a watery death there as sun-bleached bones dotted the area around the hole. Foxes were blamed for some sheep killings but were spotted infrequently in our area. I left and returned to join the search for the other sheep.

I found my father and brothers on the south side of the hill, where they had located most of our flock. My father stood on a slight rise with our dog Beara by his side. With a shrill whistle from my father, Beara swept into action. He sprinted around the fleeing sheep and forced them downhill. Another whistle of a different tone stopped him dead in his tracks, allowing the panic-stricken sheep some breathing space. Beara sometimes got a bit carried away with the thrill of the chase and nipped the heels of some stragglers. He proved his worth in rounding up sheep numerous times and was indispensable to us.

I watched the sheep run blindly in all directions and shook my head at their nervous nature. I couldn't help but compare them to cows. Cows were big, lovable fools with bulging bellies, large trusting eyes, and tongues they could stick up their noses. I imagined there wasn't much going on behind their soft, docile eyes. Sheep were a different matter. They were extremely skittish and their expression was of a constant state of shock, or expecting to be shocked. Even when contentedly chewing grass, they were wide-eyed with fright.

As the flock made their way down the hill road, I noticed that many of them had long fleeces matted with briars and parts of furze bushes. They would have to be shorn soon, I thought gloomily. Shearing is one of the hardest jobs associated with sheep and one that I was keen to minimise my involvement with. At shearing time, the flock were gathered into the Dipping Tank. My father and brothers used hand shears, which required strong arms. They worked in silence, each bent over a sheep as the shears cut through the fleece, slowly parting it from its owner. The sound of the metallic clippers slicing through the wool was the only sound heard above the chorus of bleating sheep. At the end of the day, we usually had a small mountain of wool to carry home. After throwing the last fleece onto the trailer, I loved to jump aboard and sink into the comfort of a bed of wool. I was no fan of shearing but this made up for it. Not even the jarring journey down the hill road could take away from the bliss of resting on a trailer full of wool.

Along with the flock were the lambs, over three months old by then. They had grown big and sturdy since they were born. Lambing season was one of the highlights of the farming year. Within weeks of the first one appearing around the end of February, the fields around the house were dotted with snowy-fleeced lambs. These playful creatures, gambling and racing each other around the meadow, were one of nature's most joyful sights and the signal that spring had finally arrived.

However, it was also a dangerous time for the young lambs as they were vulnerable to attacks from dogs or the odd fox. A neighbour's dog once attacked some lambs in our flock, killing one and badly wounding another three. Once a dog has tasted blood, he was sure to attack again. We informed our neighbour of what happened and he nodded, knowing what had to be done. A few days later, Finbarr reported that he had seen the same dog, this time tied to a concrete block at the bottom of the river.

Sometimes, we were allowed to keep a lamb as a pet if its mother died. My sisters had adopted one such pet lamb the previous year and named him Cottontail. He became a firm favourite with all the family. My sisters fed him bottles of milk near the fire at every opportunity.

He followed them around the yard like a puppy, bleating and looking for more milk. My sister Fiona wanted to go to a fancy dress competition in the village hall and wanted to bring Cottontail. She tied a bright red bow around his neck and went as "Mary and Her Little Lamb". Once they got to the hall, swarms of adoring children engulfed Cottontail, wanting to pet him. The excitement was too much for little Cottontail and he left a mighty pool of pee and dung in the middle of the hall, much to the amusement of the parents. It was hard to believe that The Beast that attacked me could have started life as a playful lamb similar to our own Cottontail.

As we neared the shed, Beara instinctively stopped running and crouched down low, watching the sheep. This allowed the frightened flock time to relax a little and find their way up the lane. Once near the open door of the shed, we closed in around them and forced them inside. Beara sat bolt upright outside the door, vigilant for any opportunistic breakouts while accepting the pats and praise heaped on him for a job well done. His work for the finished, I tied him up and gave him some well-deserved food and water.

I returned to the shed to lend a hand with the dosing. Dosing protected the sheep against a range of internal worms and parasites. I guarded the open doorway while my father waded into the flock, sheep parting before him like the Red Sea had done for Moses. Once he grabbed a sheep, he immediately sat it on its rump with its mouth facing upwards. When instructed, my brother David filled a plastic bottle with the right amount of dose and handed it to my father. Holding the sheep between his knees, he took the bottle and jammed into the sheep's mouth, forcing the contents down its throat. While my father held the sheep, David painted a blue mark in the middle of its back. This mark identified our sheep from the others that wandered the hill. Once done, David passed me the sheep and I released it to the freedom of the meadow. Beara strained on his leash with a confused look as they dashed past him, unsure if this exodus was sanctioned or the mass breakout he had always feared.

This system was working fine until my father approached an enormous ram. He wasn't ours and my father attempted to separate him from the rest of the sheep. He was huge in comparison to the others. Shears hadn't touched his unruly mane of wool in years. His thick horns curled menacing on either side of his head; two black patches covered his eyes to match his dark muzzle; and his nostrils flared like hot steam. His bulging eyes were dark as a bottomless well and balls of dung dangled from his rump in impressive quantities.

While other sheep melted away on my father's approach, The Beast stood his ground, staring dead ahead and breathing hard. Even my father seemed unsure of how to tackle him. Before he could make a grab for him, it happened. The Beast bolted past my father's flailing grasp and ran directly for the doorway where I stood. He ran towards freedom as if I wasn't there and, in a few seconds, I wasn't. The impact of his thick horns knocked me clean off my feet. The blow threw me into the air and I landed right on his back. I was so startled by the speed of events that I hardly realised that The Beast was carrying me along as he burst out the door.

"Jesus Christ, why didn't you block him?" my father yelled as he saw the monster carrying me out of the shed. I had no sooner gotten over the initial shock, when The Beast shook me unceremoniously from his back and onto the dusty ground. However, he wasn't finished yet.

Instead of fleeing into the meadow, The Beast turned into the yard in front of the house. David and my father surrounded him and attempted to force him back into the shed. From the look of terror on their faces, they might as well have been trying to capture a lion. The Beast charged at my brother who, after seeing what happened to me, wisely jumped aside rather than end up with a pair of sore knees. Beara was tied up in his doghouse and barking furiously at the commotion. He strained at his leash and itched to join the fight. He wouldn't have to wait long — the fight would come to him. The Beast ran past our barking bog before stopping dead in his tracks and fixing him with "The Stare". I recognised that cold look and knew what was coming next. The Beast turned and charged directly at Beara. The tormentor was about to become the tormented. Poor Beara howled as he was rammed a number of times by The Beast. Once he had punished the dog enough, The Beast turned and fled. My father had seen enough of this animal and opened the field gate, allowing him to race unhindered into the meadow.

Rubbing my sore knees, I watched with relief as The Beast trundled across the field. He stopped briefly to glance back at me before bursting across the river and disappearing towards the hill. We never saw him again or discovered who owned him. Every time we gathered sheep after that, we watched to see if he among them but he never was. The experience chastened our dog Beara and he was never as hard on sheep after that. My encounter with The Beast had shattered a long-held stereotype. Not all sheep were as meek as lambs. Some were wolves in sheep's clothing.

4 CUTTING THE TURF

My father moved with a rhythmic motion as he sliced through the soft bog and scooped the black sods onto the bank. Slice and thud, slice and thud — that was the soundtrack to a day cutting the turf. Bending his knees, he pushed the sleán into the bog and swung the peat onto the bank in one motion. A cool breeze blew across the open hill, bowing the heads of delicate bog cotton and making me shiver in my sweat-soaked shirt. I tried not to think about how long it would be until lunch and bent my back to the work again. Cutting turf was always a long and hungry day.

We usually started the long process of harvesting turf in early April, when the bogs were dry enough to allow a tractor access them. When the day looked fine, my father roused me early from my bed, telling me to get ready to go at the turf. We had some bogs in a coarse field across the river but the best stuff was on the hill. After breakfast, I helped my brothers load tools and supplies into the trailer before climbing aboard. Our tractor was a red Massey Ferguson that seemed to have been on the farm forever. She was a real workhorse and had made many journeys to the bog. As we fought over the best spot on the trailer to sit in, my mother came out with two large bags filled with food. She also gave us three large flasks of hot black tea. No trip to the bog was ever undertaken without a good supply of life-reviving tea. Once everything was loaded up, my father started the tractor on its journey to the hill.

The trip usually took about half an hour, the last twenty minutes a bone-jarring ride up the badly rutted hill road. As the tractor rattled higher into the hill, I admired the panoramic view of the Inches valley, with the lovely Coulagh Bay to the west. Splashes of purple heather added colour to the hill, as did many delicate wild flowers. The noisy tractor startled a hare, sending him sprinting across the hillside. The engine laboured until we reached the shoulder of the hill and descended to the south side, Inches disappearing from view behind me. Shortly after, my father ordered us off the trailer as he put the tractor in low gear and carefully guided it into the bogs. If one route proved too boggy, he reversed the tractor and attempted another path. It took the concentration and skill of a ship's captain to guide the tractor safely though the sea of swampy bogs. Even though we shared the hill with other farmers, everyone had their own section of bogland. When we reached ours, we unloaded the gear and wasted no time in getting to work.

My father grabbed the hay-knife and started to "skin" the bog. This meant removing the top layer of the ground, mostly just grass and earth that couldn't be used for fuel. Once this top sod was removed, my father then started to cut the turf. He used a two-sided spade called a sleán (pronounced sch-lawn), a tool designed specifically for cutting turf. As the sods landed on the dry bank, I worked with my brothers to toss them further out with a two-pronged pike. We did this to ensure each sod could dry without piling up on each other.

When my father cut turf, he was completely focused on the job. It was as if he was in a trance as he pierced the black bog with the sleán and slung each sod onto the bank without looking. His steady pace never relented and we struggled to keep up as we spread the sods. As the day wore on, he moved deeper into the bog until he eventually disappeared from view. Only the constant stream of turf spewing from the ground indicated he was still there.

While digging, he sometimes hit stumps of bog pine. These were the near-fossilised remains of ancient pine trees that once covered Ireland over three thousand years ago. Forests were so extensive in those times that it was said a squirrel could cross Ireland without touching the ground. The bog pine was reddish in colour and as hard as rock. The previous year, we brought a stump home for the fire. However, the wood was so dense that it nearly blunted our saw trying to cut it up. In addition to these pieces of wood, well-preserved human remains from ancient times were discovered in Irish bogs. We never found any bodies in our bog but many were sunburnt there.

After a few hours digging the turf, it was time for lunch. This was my favourite part of a day at the bog. We picked out a nice piece of dry ground for our picnic. I retrieved the bottle of milk immersed in a hole of bog water. This kept it cold during the heat of the day. We used this milk for the tea. I opened the lunch bag my mother gave us to reveal decks of sandwiches made with thick slices of homemade brown bread, layered with butter and filled with bacon, chicken and lettuce. There were also some custard cream biscuits for a snack. My father passed each of us a cup of steaming tea and we devoured our food happily, basking in the warm sun.

"In my day, we had to make a fire here to boil water for the tea," my father said, in between mouthfuls of food. "We had no flasks to keep things hot. We brought our kettle with us and made a fire to boil the water. Everyone did the same, so you could see columns of smoke from all the fires across our hill and Knockoura," he said, pointing to a mountain to the west.

From our spot, we had a splendid view of the Beara Peninsula. To the south lay the sheltered harbour of Berehaven, with the fishing port of Castletownbere nestled on one side and the protective hulk of Bere Island on the other. On a clear day, you could see the neighbouring peninsula of Sheep's Head. As I enjoyed my last sandwich, I watched a fishing trawler leaving the shelter of Berehaven. It chugged towards the mouth of the harbour, passing the lighthouse and ruins of Dunboy Castle before entering the wild Atlantic. I watched it until it disappeared behind Bere Island.

The hill was a great place to get away from things and be on your own. Some days, I wandered up to there and just rambled about it with no particular direction in mind. I enjoyed hiking up to the small lake at the very top before descending to the rocky glen on the opposite side. I could be alone with my thoughts and enjoy the wonderful scenery around me. It was a way to clear my head as I traipsed over the boggy ground. Away from the distractions of life, I could sit on a dry piece of ground and just stare up at the clouds flying by. There was a peace and calm in the hill that you couldn't find elsewhere. It was a place to recharge before returning to life in the lowlands once more.

Once we finished the sandwiches, my father rose wordlessly and returned to the bog. Sighing, I picked up my pike and got back to work. We continued the process of cutting and spreading the turf for the next few hours. The bog was a very slippery place to work. Wet peat stuck to the soles of your boots and you could easily end up on your arse if you weren't careful. After a while, sods of turf completely filled the bank, scattered like dead soldiers after a battle. After hours of toil, my father uttered the words I longed to hear: "That'll do for today." Letting out a sigh of relief, I straightened my aching back and gathered the tools into the trailer. We made the journey home in silence, everyone tired after the day. Inches came into view once more as we descended the northern side of the hill. The blazing sun had transformed into an orange ball as it disappeared behind Scarriff Island in Coulagh Bay and set the sky on fire. It was a spectacular end to a busy day.

After a week of good weather, the turf dried from its soggy beginnings into a semi-hard state. Then it was time to organise it for further drying. We returned to the bog to start the second phase. We created little pyramids of turf by standing five or six sods upright and leaning them against each other. This way, the turf received maximum exposure to the sun and wind. This process was called "footing the turf" and was the most labour-intensive as it involved a lot of bending over. During a short break for tea, my father pointed to a raised piece of bog in the middle of a marshy area of the hill.

"Irish freedom fighters used to hide guns there during the War of Independence in the 1920s," he said. It was a perfect hiding place, like a tiny island on a boggy lake. After our tea break, we continued footing the turf for another few hours until it was time to go home. We returned to the bog over the followings days until all the turf was footed.

When it was sufficiently dry, the turf had to be bagged before being brought home. We filled old fertilizer and cattle-feed bags with the hard black sods. It was important to get as much bagged as possible while the weather was good. This ensured that if it rained, the turf in the bags would be kept dry.

Once all the turf was safely bagged, it was ready to be brought home. Getting the tractor into the bog was one thing, but getting it out with a heavy load of turf was another. If the weather had been wet, then there was a real danger of the tractor wheels sinking in the bog and getting stuck. To avoid this, my father often left the tractor by the hill-road while we carted the bags of turf out to it using a wheelbarrow.

"Footing" the turf in the hill

It took many trips from the house to the hill to get the turf home. My father tipped the contents of each trailer load outside the turf shed before returning to the hill. While he was gone, I helped my brother David draw the bags into the shed where they would be dry for the winter.

Saving the turf was hard work but healthy and rewarding with days spent in the fresh air. It also gave us the benefit of our own independent source of fuel. The earth had yielded its natural resources. For the rest of the year, we had a shed full of dry turf to use. It warmed the kitchen where we gathered to eat. It cooked our meals, baked the bread for our school lunches, and dried our clothes after a rainy day. Harvesting the turf may have been a long and hard road but it was well worth it.

Digging
By Seamus Heaney

Between my finger and my thumb
The squat pen rests; as snug as a gun.

Under my window a clean rasping sound
When the spade sinks into gravelly ground:
My father, digging. I look down

Till his straining rump among the flowerbeds
Bends low, comes up twenty years away
Stooping in rhythm through potato drills
Where he was digging.

The coarse boot nestled on the lug, the shaft
Against the inside knee was levered firmly.
He rooted out tall tops, buried the bright edge deep
To scatter new potatoes that we picked
Loving their cool hardness in our hands.

By God, the old man could handle a spade,
Just like his old man.
My grandfather could cut more turf in a day
Than any other man on Toner's bog.
Once I carried him milk in a bottle
Corked sloppily with paper. He straightened up
To drink it, then fell to right away
Nicking and slicing neatly, heaving sods
Over his shoulder, digging down and down
For the good turf. Digging.

The cold smell of potato mold, the squelch and slap
Of soggy peat, the curt cuts of an edge
Through living roots awaken in my head.
But I've no spade to follow men like them.

Between my finger and my thumb
The squat pen rests.
I'll dig with it.

5 MY VERY OWN OGHAM STONE

The bell above the shop door tinkled to announce our arrival to the small shop. I was helping my grandmother buy some gifts for Christmas. For a sixteen-year-old boy, it was a chore but also gave me the chance to suggest some purchases for her favourite grandson. She knew Eileen, the shop owner and it was as much a social call as a shopping visit. They chatted about old friends, dead neighbours, and distant sons and daughters. I feigned interest in some jewellery behind a glass casing while they talked.

"We found one on your land Lena, one which the Historical Society didn't know about," Eileen said to my grandmother. "I was searching for a holy well there a few weeks ago when I came across it." Eileen seemed excited by this discovery. "There's an expert coming down from Cork City next month to examine it," she revealed, too excited to explain exactly what she had found. Eileen was a member of the local historical society, an organisation dedicated to recording all the ancient monuments of the Beara Peninsula.

"It could be over a thousand years old," she continued, barely pausing to draw breath. My grandmother placed a gentle hand on her arm to calm her.
"What did you say you found at all, girl?" she asked.
"A previously undiscovered Ogham stone, Lena," she replied with glee. My Gran wasn't impressed and let her hand drop from Eileen's arm in disappointment.
"Wisha, is that all?" she said, before following up. "And what is an Ogham stone anyway?"

I listened to this discussion in stunned silence. The mention of the Ogham stone had triggered some long-forgotten memories and brought them flooding back, memories which I hoped and prayed hadn't come back to haunt me.

* * *

After Kilmacowen School closed in 1978, I started in Eyeries National School. It was a fine modern building and had all the facilities that Kilmacowen lacked such as electricity and running water. When I was ten-years-old, I developed a peculiar interest in Ogham stones. Our teacher Mr. Lynch taught us about the ancient Ogham stones of Ireland. During the course of the class, I learned that these standing stones could be found dotted around the country and contained inscriptions in Ogham, an ancient Gaelic script. Ogham used a series of lines to represent a sound or letter, which were engraved along the edge of the stone. This ancient script had only been deciphered in the last hundred years and many inscriptions had only recently been translated. No one was sure what the stones were meant to serve as or signify. Some say they were landmarks for sailors. Others say the stones marked the graves of important chiefs or warriors. Whatever the reason for them, I was completely fascinated.

Mr. Lynch told us that Ogham first appeared in Ireland around two thousand years ago but is probably far older than that. The inscriptions normally recorded facts about a member of a tribe. Druids also used it for recording tales, histories, poetry, and genealogies. The name Ogham was derived from the Celtic god of literature and eloquence, Ogma. An individual letter contained one to five vertical or angled lines. Ogham was read from top to bottom and from left to right. In keeping with the Druidic ways and their love of nature, each of Ogham's twenty letters bears the name of a tree — A-Ailim (Elm), B-Bithe (Birch), and C-Coll (Hazel) for example. Ogham stones can be found not only in Ireland but also sporadically across Scotland, the Isle of Man, Wales, and England.

The fact that the tallest Ogham Stone in Western Europe stood only a few miles from my home only served to deepen my interest. When I visited the Ballycrovane Ogham Stone for the first time, I hadn't been prepared for something so big. It was over seventeen feet tall and commanded an impressive view of the lovely Ballycrovane harbour. The Ogham inscription on the Ballycrovane Stone read:

"MAQI DECCADDA SAFI TORAIN AS"

This has been translated as, "son of Decada, from the warriors of Turain." This could have been the grave of a warrior chief or a memorial stone to him. Whatever the reason, the person whose name was etched on the Ballycrovane stone had become immortal. His name was being discussed almost a thousand years after he had died. I found this amazing. I wanted desperately to try to experience some of that immortality that he had attained. I decided there and then to make my very own Ogham stone. Now, I had of course no intention of erecting a seventeen-foot high stone to rival the great memorial of Ballycrovane. All I wanted was something simple but the problem was where to find a suitable standing stone for the task.

Ballycrovane Ogham Stone

Stone walls formed the boundary of many fields on our farm. Constructed generations before, they required maintenance to avoid dilapidation and damage from cattle. In one small field above the house, the wall had been removed, leaving only the four-foot high support stones. One of these remaining pillars would prove ideal for my project. I selected a lichen-covered stone with nice straight edges to work with. Situated on a little rise just above the house, it commanded a sweeping view of Coulagh Bay, studded with the islands of Inishfarnard and Scariff. It was a perfect setting for my project.

I borrowed my father's hammer and chisel and went to work. The hard iron of the chisel cut into the stone with every blow of the hammer, leaving a line behind. I chiselled over each groove numerous times to leave an incision deep enough to last the test of time. The clang of the hammer on the chisel rang out across the windswept fields, a handful of sheep the only curious onlookers. I worked all day through the hard stone until I had carved out a number of lines on the edge of the rock. I stood back to inspect the fourteen simple lines I had inscribed. The markings translated as "Séan", the Gaelic word for John. The Ogham script has no letter "J", so I couldn't inscribe "John". I felt I was the only person in my locality, maybe even the world, to have his own Ogham stone.

Time went by and I lost interest in Ogham. I went to secondary school in Castletownbere to continue my education. Football and girls replaced my fascination with Ogham. Chiselling inscriptions on rocks seemed silly and the memory of what I had carved faded. Fast growing furze bushes soon encircled and swallowed my Ogham stone, obscuring it from view for years and seemingly consigning it to history. That was, until Eileen O'Sullivan came across it while searching for a holy well.

After I heard Eileen's announcement in the shop, I feared the worst.

"Eileen, where exactly did you find this stone?" I asked guiltily, deep in my heart already knowing the answer.
"Would you believe, it's just above your house, on a little rise," she said. "I'm surprised that none of you noticed something like that before and it right under your noses." It was time for me to confess the truth.
"Eileen, I'm afraid that Ogham stone isn't a thousand years old as I carved it myself."

You could hear a pin drop. She seemed flustered by the news but, to her credit, she managed to maintain her composure. I explained how I had carved the stone years earlier and apologised to her if my youthful fascination with Ogham had caused her any embarrassment.

"Oh well, of course, I didn't think it was that old," she muttered. "It would have been discovered by now if it was."

We gathered up our purchases and left quickly. Even though I felt bad to have caused some embarrassment, I couldn't help smiling. It looked like I wouldn't have to wait a thousand years at all to have my stone talked about — ten years did the job nicely.

A Mountaineer
by Pádraic Colum

ERE Beowulf's song
Was heard from the ships,
Ere Roland had set
The horn to his lips:

In Ogham strokes
A name was writ:
That name his name
Lives in yet.

The strokes on the edge
Of the stone might count
The acres he has
On this bare mount;

But he remembers
The pillar-stone,
And knows that he is
Of the seed of Eoin.

6 SAVING THE HAY

Great swathes of tall grass fell before each blow of the deadly scythe. My father swung the blade expertly, moving forward a few steps after each swing to allow it to reach fresh grass. Sweat flowed freely down his face as he worked. He stopped to throw off his sodden shirt and adjust his trouser-braces on his bare shoulders before replacing his trusty straw hat on his head. The edges of the hat were badly frayed and pieces of straw poked through like the broken spokes on a bicycle wheel. He picked up the scythe and started again.

After a while, he stopped again to sharpen the scythe. He told me that a well-sharpened scythe could knock a field of grass with relative ease. It had a curved wooden handle with two handgrips fitted near the centre. The sloping steel blade was attached to the end of the handle.

He placed it on the ground with the blade pointing upwards and picked up the sharpening stone. It was shaped like a foot-long cigar and had a rough texture. Wetting the stone with some water, he drew it swiftly and skilfully up and down the blade, alternating between both edges. The swish, swish sound of the stone on the blade was the music of his instrument. Cutting hay in this fashion was hard work and time consuming. Once the tractor and mechanical mower became popular, the scythe was retired to the rafters above the shed.

Cutting and saving the hay was an important part of the farming season and ensured a food supply for the cattle and sheep during the winter. In order to allow the grass grow for the hay, fields had to be blocked off from the cattle in the spring. In April, we spread cow dung to encourage a rich growth. The grass grew tall and lush a month after the spreading. This sight was too tempting for the cattle that sometimes managed to break into the meadow through a weak part of the fence. They gorged themselves on the grass before we discovered them and drove them out of the meadow with lashings of the stick.

The odd invasion apart, the grass grew uninterrupted. The end of June or early July was deemed the best time to cut the hay. We hired a local contractor named Richard Power to cut the hay for us. His powerful tractor rumbled into the yard like a tank, scattering hens in all directions. It was armed with the mechanical mower at the back, which consisted of a long upright arm, studded with rows of serrated steel teeth. Once he drove the tractor into the meadow, Richard unfolded the mower. After a few adjustments, he started the tractor and the teeth of the mower burst into life, felling all before it.

The mower moved around the perimeter of the meadow and worked its way inwards. The beautiful smell of freshly cut grass perfumed the summer air. Once the meadow was cut, the mower moved onto the neighbouring field of Beart Beag (Little Parcel). The Gaelic names of some fields had survived even after the spoken language had ceased in the area for over a century. Once Richard finished the cutting, he usually stopped into the kitchen for a quick bite to eat. This was a busy time for him so he never delayed, quickly finishing off a sandwich and mug of tea before jumping into his tractor to cut the next farmer's field.

Once the mower had gone, my father instructed the children to go around the meadow and pick out as many thistles and cupógs (dock weeds) as possible. The cupógs were rusty coloured weeds and were bad for cattle if left in the hay.

The grass was allowed to dry for a day or two before it had to be turned. My father and two brothers each took a two-pronged pike from the shed before starting. My heart sank when I stood on top of the meadow and saw the magnitude of the task ahead. An ocean of grass lay before me and it all had to be turned by hand. I got stuck into the work and kept my head down, turning and shaking out the hay into rows. Bit by bit, we started making inroads into the meadow, steadily shrinking the amount left to do. I was lost with my own thoughts as I worked, mechanically turning each batch of hay as the sun beat down.

As we toiled at turning and shaking out the hay, the sweetest sound we could hear was the sharp blast of an old whistle. On hearing this, I snapped out of my daydreams to see my grandmother standing at the top of the meadow in her blue floral apron, blowing the whistle to call us to lunch. The whistle was a sort of family heirloom and had been in the house for decades. It was battered but still able to emit an ear-piercing blast. I heard its sweet call on many occasions while working in the fields or at the bog across the river. It was a relief to hear its shrill call, announcing a break from raking the hay or footing the turf.

Once we finished our food, I returned to the meadow with a heavy heart. There was much more work left to do. As before, I put these thoughts out of my head and turned the first batch of hay. As I worked, I saw our neighbours were also turning hay in their fields across the river. From Bawnard to Mileens, people were working at the hay, some turning while others were already making haystacks.

Slowly, the unturned part of the meadow shrank until I finally linked up with my father and brothers in the middle of the field. We had literally turned the meadow from green to yellow. I slouched back to the house after the long day, tired and with blistered hands. We repeated this task many times over the following days, the hay changing to a golden yellow colour in the process. Drying the hay didn't always go according to plan, however.

Farmers are at the mercy of the weather and for many years, we were blessed with fine weather in which to save the hay. On other years, however, we weren't so lucky and it rained for weeks after the fields were cut. It was impossible to turn the hay when the weather was so bad. During a brief dry spell, we turned as much as we could before fresh showers forced us to abandon the work. There was nothing we could do but watch the hay turn black and rot. An air of depression hung about the house for weeks after and everyone had short tempers. It was a heart-breaking sight to see a field of black rows instead of golden ones.

Thankfully, losing the hay like that was rare. Once it was dry enough, we had to make the hay into haystacks or "cocks". This involved gathering it into piles about eight feet high. I loved to stand on top of the cock of hay and trample it down. Loose hay was raked off the sides until it formed a smooth mound. Once that was done, my father threw a square cover over the top of the haystack and told me to secure each corner to the base with twine. He warned me to make sure the knots in the twine faced outwards so any rain would drip away from the hay. This covering kept the hay dry until it could be brought into the hayshed.

If we were too busy to come into the house for lunch, my mother brought it out to us in the meadow. This suited me fine as I preferred eating in the meadow anyway. Sitting on a half-made haystack, we enjoyed our sandwiches and tea. It was the most comfortable seat I ever sat in and it was very hard to get up from once the food was finished. By the end of the day, the meadow was dotted with cocks of hay. We played hide and seek behind them for the remainder of the evening. We also loved jumping into the haystacks, pretending to be stuntmen in an action movie. It was a natural playground for us. We played in the meadow until it was dark.

Eventually, the haystacks had to be brought in from the meadow and stored near the house. We used the horse and cart to do this before we purchased a tractor. Once the hay was piled onto the cart, my father secured it with a rope. I then climbed on top of the load for the journey home. I held onto the rope as the horse drew the load of hay home. It was a great feeling to be looking down on the world from such a lofty height.

My father and grandfather bringing in the hay

Once the load was home, we used it to create a mountain of hay called a "reek". This was made in the same way as a haystack but on a much bigger scale. Two people stood on top of the reek as others piked hay up to them. The ones on top had to distribute the hay evenly and trample it down. This was done to expel as much air as possible from the reek. As it got higher, we used a ladder to pike up the last load. It was a bit scary to be on top of the full reek, looking down at people far below. It was also great fun to slide down off the side although we were warned not to.

When possible, we tried to have the hay saved for the Regatta during the August Bank Holiday in Castletownbere. The Regatta was the biggest festival of the summer and meant amusements such as swinging boats, bumper cars and ice-cream cones. Everyone was anxious to be finished with the hay for the Regatta so we could enjoy ourselves. With this in mind, we worked hard at the hay leading up the Regatta. A new hayshed had replaced the reek in later years. My father brought the hay in from the fields using the tractor and trailer and dumped it outside the hayshed. I worked with my brothers to pike it inside and make room for the other loads. As with the reek, we stood down on the hay to compact it. As more hay was piled into the shed, we rose higher and higher until we had to stoop down under the rafters. The heat was stifling and sweat poured freely down my face. After my father delivered the final load, everyone helped to pack it until my father finally closed the doors of the hayshed. We had saved the hay and everyone breathed a sigh of relief. As fast as I could, I dumped my pike in the cabin and ran off to join my brothers for a well-deserved swim in the river.

That night, I searched myself for sceartáns, small ticks from the hay that embedded themselves in our skin. I usually found four or five of these sceartáns after a day at the hay. They had to be swiftly pulled from the skin to avoid their heads breaking off. If that happened, it became very itchy. Some escaped this initial detection, only to be found days later having grown fat on my blood.

In later years, more machinery was involved in the haymaking. One year, we hired a mechanical hay turner and it did in an hour what would have taken us a whole day to accomplish. The following year, we hired a mechanical hay baler. It gobbled up the rows of hay and spat them out as tightly bound blocks. Even though the machinery made saving the hay much easier, it turned us into mere spectators. No longer did we cut the grass or turn the hay, machines did it all for us. Nobody missed the days of hard work, but it did leave a gap in the summer where cocks of golden hay should have been.

The baler became an annual visitor to our farm. One summer after completing its work, I stood at the gate and counted the bales scattered across the meadow. All the hay had been baled that year except for one small field that the mechanical mower couldn't access due to a narrow gap. I noticed my father working in that field. He was stripped to the waist with his trouser-braces on his bare shoulders, wearing his frayed straw hat. The old scythe swung back and forth in his hands, felling large swathes of grass as he smiled contentedly.

7 THE GREEN GARDEN

Lamb chops sizzled on the frying pan before my mother dished them out to us. The chops were golden brown and smothered with fried onions. They were soon joined on the plate by my mother's delicious turnip mash, which I could have eaten on its own for dinner. Finally, a big plate of steaming potatoes was placed in the middle of the table, their jackets peeling off. Once the potatoes were served, we could start eating. The potatoes occupied the centre of the table, with everything else revolving around them.

"Fine floury ones this year," my mother commented as I took a potato and peeled the skin off. I mashed mine up with butter and salt to make the loveliest mash. My father ate his with the skins still on.

"That's where the goodness is," he claimed. With or without their skins, potatoes were a key part of our diet and a meal wasn't complete unless it was accompanied with potatoes.

A lot of work went into them before they arrived at the table. We usually chose a field near the river called the Garra Glas (Green Garden) to plant the potatoes. The old Gaelic name was very apt as the soil there was rich and fertile. Using a spade, my father dug up sods to create a ridge about a hundred feet long. I followed in his wake, "dressing" the ridges with earth dug from the furrows. He kept digging until he had two or three ridges cut through the field.

Leaning on his spade during a short break, he waited for me to catch up.

"When I was your age, I worked with my father in this field with the horse and plough," he said, wiping sweat from his forehead. "With the horse pulling it, he guided the heavy iron plough and turned up the ridges. I followed behind him, heaping earth on the ridges. He had a great eye and kept the plough dead straight, which wasn't easy."

He gazed into the distance in silence, reliving memories of a time long gone. "Hardly anybody uses a horse and plough anymore," he said regretfully, before spitting into his hands and starting back to the digging again. It was hard work and it might take a week to dig all the ridges. Once we had them made, we added cow dung on top of the ridges as fertilizer. Sometimes, we added mineral-rich seaweed, collected from the shore of Coulagh Bay.

Once the ridges were ready, the potatoes could be planted. During the previous few months, we had saved a batch of seed potatoes for planting. The most common varieties were Kerr Pink, King Edward and Rooster. They were kept in a dark part of the shed to encourage them to sprout. Each potato developed growth buds or "eyes". Sometimes, if one potato had a number of "eyes", it was split in two to create two seeds. We called these seed potatoes sciolláns. We planted the early crop in late February and the main crop in May. When they were ready for planting, we placed the sciolláns in a bucket and brought them to the ridges. We planted three of them in a row on the ridge before moving on to plant another three. My father dug the hole with a spade and I dropped the sciollán in, with the eye pointing upwards. Crows were persistent pests and we used a rough scarecrow to keep them at bay, often with some of their dead comrades hanging from each arm.

After a few weeks, the first shoots of the early potatoes appeared, slowly obscuring the brown earth. I spent many days on my knees weeding the potatoes to allow them to prosper. When the stalks were about a foot high, they were ready for "earthing". This involved digging earth from the furrow and heaping it around the potato stalk. This helped support the growing shoot and prevented sunlight getting at the potatoes. If that happened, the potatoes turned green and became poisonous. Despite the hard work, it felt good to be in contact with the earth. Squatting in the furrows with the potato stalks swaying in the breeze, I was in my own world.

When the stalks were about two feet high, they were sprayed to protect them against blight, a disease that would destroy the entire crop if not treated. Blight ruined the Irish potato harvest of 1845-1847 and ultimately caused the death of over a million people. My father transported a large wooden barrel from the shed to the Garra Glas in the back of the tractor. I filled the barrel with bucket after bucket of water from the river until it was nearly full. My father then mixed it with a concoction of washing soda and bluestone to make a bright green fungicide. He then donned his waterproof "oilskins" and poured the mixture into a mechanical knapsack sprayer, which strapped onto his back like a backpack. He walked backwards along the furrows to avoid getting wet, pumping a lever at the side of the tank that sent the spray through a rubber hose he held in his hand. He sprayed two ridges at a time, alternating from side to side. The sprayer leaked and, despite the oilskins, he was soaked through by the end of the day.

The early crop was ready for harvesting in May. Using spades, we slashed the potato stalks a few inches above the ground. Care was needed when digging, as we didn't want to cut any of the precious potatoes. This was the moment of truth when we discovered what kind of crop we had. Each time I dug up the ridge, white potatoes burst forth and tasted daylight for the first time. They were cool in my hands and had smooth skin, like the eggs of some underground creature that had abandoned her nest. It was satisfying to see what the soil could produce with hard work. In addition to potatoes, we also planted turnips, carrots, and onions in the Garra Glas so it really lived up to its name.

We planted the main potato crop soon after. The cycle of weeding, earthing and spraying was done as before. Unlike the "earlies", the main crop stayed in the ground until the stalks had withered by October. This was done to "set" the potato skins so they could be stored over the winter. The crop was darker and the skins thicker that the "earlies". There was an unofficial competition between us children as to who would unearth the biggest spud. I found a real monster one year and was thrilled when I pulled it from the earth and held it aloft for the others to see. My aunt Peggy was visiting from America at the time and took a photo of me holding my prize potato, smiling broadly. Even though we valued the big ones, we gathered every potato, no matter how small. What wasn't used for our table would be cooked and fed to the chickens.

Some potatoes had clearly rotted as pus-like slime seeped from them when squeezed. This was the work of blight. Even after spraying, some potatoes were doomed. A successful potato crop was considered a generous act of God as the potato field was at the mercy of changing weather, blight, and hungry crows. There was much outside a farmer's control and he learned to respect and read the weather and conditions as best he could. Once we had a ridge dug up, we retraced our steps and loaded the potatoes into a wheelbarrow to be brought to the potato pit. This was a shallow pit about a foot deep used to store our crop. We filled the pit and piled it high with potatoes before covering it with rushes.

Once the crop was saved, my father brought me along on the tractor when he gave bags of fresh potatoes to the neighbours. This was the traditional way of telling people that we enjoyed a good, healthy harvest. I liked to think that they enjoyed the fruit of the fields in the same way that we did. When we got home later that evening, I walked into the kitchen and could smell bacon boiling in the pot. Another pot of potatoes boiled alongside it. The meat may change but the main dish will always be the same.

Spraying the Potatoes
by Patrick Kavanagh

The barrels of blue potato-spray
Stood on a headland in July
Beside an orchard wall where roses
Were young girls hanging from the sky.

The flocks of green potato stalks
Were blossom spread for sudden flight,
The Kerr's Pinks in frivelled blue,
The Arran Banners wearing white.

And over that potato-field
A lazy veil of woven sun,
Dandelions growing on headlands, showing
Their unloved hearts to everyone.

And I was there with a knapsack sprayer
On the barrel's edge poised. A wasp was floating
Dead on a sunken briar leaf
Over a copper-poisoned ocean.

The axle-roll of a rut-locked cart
Broke the burnt stick of noon in two.
An old man came through a cornfield
Remembering his youth and some Ruth he knew.

He turned my way. 'God further the work'.
He echoed an ancient farming prayer.
I thanked him. He eyed the potato drills.
He said: 'You are bound to have good ones there'.

We talked and our talk was a theme of kings,
A theme for strings. He hunkered down
In the shade of the orchard wall. O roses
The old man dies in the young girl's frown.

And poet lost to potato-fields,
Remembering the lime and copper smell
Of the spraying barrels he is not lost
Or till blossomed stalks cannot weave a spell.

8 TILL THE COWS COME HOME

"What kept you?" the cows seemed to say to me. Their heads rested on top of the gate, flapping their ears and swatting flies nonchalantly with their tails. I was supposed to have driven them to the shed for milking an hour earlier so they were annoyed that I kept them waiting. Some had udders so full, milk squirted from their teats as they walked. They bellowed at me impatiently as I opened the gate and released them. Relieved to be finally underway, they ambled up the lane towards the shed. They needed no coercion, as they knew the routine. I stayed well behind them as I followed them up the lane to the house. Experience had taught me that if I walked behind them too closely, they were likely to suddenly lift a tail and spew watery dung in my direction. The cows had their own names like Crowley's Cow, named after her former owner; the

Strawberry Cow, named after her distinctive red markings; and Finbarr's Cow, because she was Finbarr's favourite.

Once inside the shed, Finbarr helped to tether the cows in their individual stalls. I never did much milking as my father and brothers were much better at it than I was. Many cows had been giving milk for years and were used to having someone sit under them and milk them. Other cows were new to the experience and thus, were unpredictable. They tended to kick out in protest with their powerful back legs when someone attempted to milk them for the first time. These nervous cows had to have their back legs tied with a thin rope called a spancel during milking to stop them kicking. Even with their legs secured, they could still use their tails as weapons. A swinging tail, caked with hardened dung, was something we never wanted to get across the face.

One such nervous cow was the Strawberry Cow. It was her first year being milked and she didn't take to the experience well. She kicked out wildly with her back legs whenever anybody tried to milk her. She only seemed comfortable when my father did so. He sang a kind of mantra that seemed to soothe her — "rayshea, rayshea," he repeated softly as he milked her. It seemed to do the trick. My mother also sang to the cows during milking, saying that it calmed them and they gave their milk more freely.

One evening, my father was away and I was forced to milk the Strawberry Cow. I was nervous at the prospect and a cow could sense fear and react to it. I tried to calm her by repeating the mantra my father had used. "Rayshea, rayshea," I whispered as I slid the wooden stool under her and tried to tie the spancel around her back legs. It was a struggle but, after a few whacks from her tail, I managed to tie her back legs. I then started to milk her, a slow rhythmic pulling of the two back teats to start the flow. The first streams hit the aluminium bucket with a metallic zing. The sound softened as the bucket filled with foamy milk. My brother Finbarr was milking in the next stall as I got to grips with my task. The Strawberry Cow was as good as gold, chewing the cud with a rhythmic grinding of her jaws. Just as I was thinking that she wasn't so bad, she suddenly kicked out, her back leg straining on the spancel. She didn't make contact with me but I jumped back from her out of fright, stumbling over the stool and falling on my back into a heap of fresh cow dung. The contents of the bucket joined me soon after. Finbarr popped his head around to see what the commotion was and uttered a great, hearty laugh when he saw me in the drain. The Strawberry Cow wasn't going to be milked that easily.

Barring such minor disasters, once the bucket was full, I brought it up to the house and poured it into galvanised containers called creamery cans. A muslin cloth placed over the opening of each can acted as a filter to catch any debris that may have ended up in the milk. Each can had two handles on either side for carrying and held six gallons of milk. Once the cans were full, my father replaced their lids before heaving them into trailer and driving them to the nearby creamery stop. The creamery stop was a concrete platform near Kilmacowen Cross, where cans of milk were left to be collected by the Creamery Lorry. It was a busy place during collection time with farmers coming and going, chatting and swopping news. Each can had the farmer's creamery number painted on its side. When the Creamery Lorry arrived, the driver placed a large tube into each can and sucked the milk into a tank in the back of the lorry. He then recorded the number on the can into a notebook before departing. We brought our empty cans home and washed them thoroughly for use the following day.

When we had a surplus of milk, my mother made butter. She first doled the milk into shallow pails and placed them across the floor of the porch. These were left there overnight to allow the cream to rise to the top. The next day, she skimmed the cream into a metal container. The container was actually a disused sweet can that she obtained from a shop in Castletownbere. It was ideal, as we didn't require a bigger churn. Once she had enough cream in the can, she placed the lid on it and starting shaking it hard. It was tough work and she paused every five minutes for a short break before the churning continued. After a while, the sound of the cream sloshing around the can got heavier. Eventually, I heard a thudding sound as the first globs of butter formed. The sound grew until there seemed to be a few good lumps there. My mother then opened the can and extracted the lumps of butter. She washed it thoroughly with cold water and mixed it with salt before finally rolling it into balls. It was stored in the fridge to for use on bread and with cooking.

During the wet winter months, we kept the cattle in the shed at night and fed them hay or silage. During the day, they were released to roam the fields so that their stalls could be cleaned and fresh bedding put down for them. I helped my brothers to scoop the dung and old bedding to the end of the shed where it was then piked it out the window onto the dung pit. We threw fresh bedding of straw and rushes on the concrete floor for the cows before they came in for the night. Sometimes, it might be days before we cleaned the shed. By then, the bung and bedding had become hard and matted. It was hard work to just peel each layer and get it out of the window.

The dung pit filled up quickly over the winter and it needed to be spread on the fields in spring. Moving a small mountain of cow manure was a lengthy process. Using a four-pronged pike, I filled the wheelbarrow with dung and rotted bedding while my brother David carted it to the nearby meadow. He tipped the contents onto the grass before returning for a fresh load. It wasn't long before the meadow was dotted with little hills of dung. Some days later, we returned to the meadow to spread the dung, breaking up some stubborn clumps as small as possible with the pike. By the time we finished, the meadow was dark with dung. The inevitable rains dissolved the manure into the ground over the following weeks.

When cows were ready to be impregnated by the bull, they were said to be "going to dairy." We had a fine bull but kept him well away from the cows until the right time. The pedigree of bull determined the quality of calf and the price it might fetch at the fair. Not everyone had a bull and, if a farmer had a pedigree animal, the bull was in demand and could take on three or four cows in a day. It must have been a happy time for the bull as he watched the stream of visitors looking for his services.

Very little would keep a bull from the cows if "the urge" was strong enough. I woke one morning in my grandmother's house to a roar from the yard that had me out of my bed in a flash. It was the sound of an animal in serious distress and I rushed outside to see what was going on. My father was ahead of me, hurriedly pulling on his braces as he dashed outside. To our horror, we saw our bull impaled on the spikes of the gate beside the house. The cows were in that field and the temptation had been too great for him. It was a brave but doomed attempt to vault the steel-spiked gate. My father quickly got a sledgehammer and managed to blow the gate off the pillar. The poor bull was in a bad way and the vet managed to stitch him up. He survived but wasn't in much form for romance after that.

Calving time was an exciting and busy time on the farm. When a cow was expected to calf, she was brought to the shed where my father could keep an eye on her. He might have to get up three or four times during the night to check her progress. We couldn't afford to lose a calf if anything went wrong during the birth. On most occasions, nature took care of everything and we visited the shed in the morning to find a beautiful new calf.

One night, I had to help my father when a cow was calving. She was having some difficulty so we called the vet. When he arrived, he pulled on blue, plastic gloves up to his elbows and reached his arms inside the cow. After a minute of probing, he told us that the calf was facing the wrong way but he had managed to turn it around. With a lot of effort, he pulled the calf's head out. Soon after, the new calf shot out into the world. We were all relieved. After a while, the calf stood up for the first time on its new wobbly legs. After a few days, both calf and mother were allowed out into the meadow. Like the lambs, the calf had great fun running around the field, investigating flowers and small insects, and discovering the world around them. However, a cow with her new calf was dangerously unpredictable, as I had discovered some years earlier.

I was around four when one of our cows calved at the bottom of our garden. I was very keen to see the new calf and, without waiting for my mother, I walked down to the bottom of the garden. I had a facemask that I got the previous Halloween and decided to wear it to welcome the new calf. Why I thought that was a good idea, I'll never know. The poor cow was in a heightened state of alert and protective of her new offspring. When she saw this strange, hideous-looking creature toddling towards her, she must have feared for her baby. She charged at me and flung me into the air with her head. My mother saw what happened and screamed to my father, who was planting potatoes in a field near the house. He came running when he heard her screams and picked up my limp body from the garden. They thought I was seriously injured but were relieved to find I had only passed out.

* * *

Fair day was on the first Thursday of every month and this was the time to buy and sell cattle. If we had any we were hoping to sell, we had to be up early to herd them into the yard in preparation for the journey to town. The road to Castletownbere had many opportunities for the cattle to break away. Any side road or boreen (laneway) was a chance for them to deviate from the main road. I had to run ahead of the herd and make sure they didn't turn off the route. It was hard going, made worse by the wet morning. My father told us that when he was young, they drove cattle to the fair in Kenmare, a distance of thirty miles. The four miles to Castletownbere was a stroll by comparison, he laughed.

It was already busy when we reached Castletownbere. The wet morning had given way to unexpected sunshine. We found a spot for our cattle and corralled them there. Merchants had erected stalls in the Square selling clothing, boots, farm machinery, and tools. Toys and plastic machine guns were also for sale, I noted. A mobile van selling burgers and chips was being readied for a busy day. There was a great hubbub from farmers arguing and cattle bellowing.

People came with livestock from all across the Beara Peninsula. Cattle from Dursey Island had to swim across the narrow channel between that island and the mainland. Ruddy-cheeked men from the distant hills of Adrigole strode up and down the Square, their trousers held in place with twine. An itinerant man pushed past me with his old bicycle, laden with plastic bottles and bags. A powerful stench rolled off him as he passed by, muttering to himself. Shops and pubs around the square did a great trade on a fair day. Cattle trucks inched along the main street, crammed with livestock. The smell of cow dung and urine filled the air. Farmers bargained hard, pretending to turn away from an offer before hearing a better number to draw them back. The prospective buyer inspected and discussed every part of the animal during the negotiations. Once agreement was reached, the men spat into their hands and shook to seal the deal.

Late in the day, we sold our cattle to a dealer from Kenmare. We were relieved, as we didn't want to drive them back home again. My father gave us some money to buy fizzy orange and sweets while he had a well-earned drink in a bar. I called into Moriarty's shop and bought chocolate and a bottle of Fanta. When we were ready, we headed for home along the old back road. It was a lovely evening and the red sky to the west promised good weather the following day. I was tired when I got home and plopped myself onto the sofa as I told my mother the news of the day. Just as I was relaxing, I heard the bellowing from the fields and groaned — our day wasn't finished yet. The milking cows were waiting.

A Drover
by Pádraic Colum

TO MEATH of the pastures,
From wet hills by the sea,
Through Leitrim and Longford
Go my cattle and me.

I hear in the darkness
Their slipping and breathing.
I name them the bye-ways
They're to pass without heeding.

Then the wet, winding roads,
Brown bogs with black water;
And my thoughts on white ships
And the King o' Spain's daughter.

O! farmer, strong farmer!
You can spend at the fair
But your face you must turn
To your crops and your care.

And soldiers—red soldiers!
You've seen many lands;
But you walk two by two,
And by captain's commands.

O! the smell of the beasts,
The wet wind in the morn;
And the proud and hard earth
Never broken for corn;

And the crowds at the fair,
The herds loosened and blind,
Loud words and dark faces
And the wild blood behind.

(O! strong men with your best
I would strive breast to breast
I could quiet your herds
With my words, with my words.)

I will bring you, my kine,
Where there's grass to the knee;
But you'll think of scant croppings
Harsh with salt of the sea.

9 WAITING FOR CHRISTMAS

"I suppose it's time to kill one of the turkeys," my father announced in the kitchen one evening before Christmas.

I'd been waiting for those words for the past few evenings and, on hearing them, I instantly asked if I could accompany him. He agreed and, with my mother's insistence, I put on my woollen coat and joined my father outside. It was a crisp December night and I scanned the sparkling sky for shooting stars. It was a short walk up to the shed with my father's flashlight shining the way. When we got there, I flicked on the light switch. In the corner of the shed was the coop containing five turkeys. My father squatted down and scanned it for a worthy bird to grace the Christmas table. He then opened the small door of the coop and pulled out the most suitable one. Strangely, the turkey came out with very little protest. We led her into the adjoining cabin. There, my father placed a wooden block in the middle of the concrete floor and picked up the sharpened axe that lay nearby. Even though I was only eight, I knew what was coming next. I'd already witnessed the slaughter of a pig and a sheep. Killing an animal for the table was part of life on the farm.

Before he positioned the turkey on the block, I cleared my throat and asked my father if I could deliver the killer blow. He seemed a bit surprised by my request but nodded his consent before handing me the axe. Stroking the turkey to keep it calm, he pressed its long neck on the block and gave me the nod. The axe suddenly felt heavy in my sweaty palms and I thought about passing it back to my father. Instead, I swallowed hard and swung the axe down on its neck. The blow wasn't hard enough to sever the turkey's neck and it squawked horribly before breaking free from my father's grasp, blood pouring from the terrible wound in its neck. I dropped the axe and my father cursed, trying to grab the dying bird as it fluttered wildly, its dark blood spraying everywhere. Its piercing shrieks reverberated around the bare walls of the cabin. When he finally got hold of the turkey, he placed its neck on the wooden block again and severed its head with one blow, silencing its cries forever. Its wings twitched for a few seconds before they were finally still. My father didn't say anything to me and I just returned to the house with my head bowed.

My father delivered the dead turkey to my mother in the kitchen shortly afterwards. She placed the bird on the table and started plucking the feathers from its still-warm body. The soft feathers from its breast were easy to extract unlike those on the wings. They were tough and demanded extra attention from my mother's strong and skilled hands. Once plucked clean, the turkey was stored until the night before Christmas Day when it would be cleaned out and readied for the dinner.

The Christmas cake was second only to the turkey in pride of place at the Christmas dinner. My mother made the cake in late November and was an early indicator of the upcoming celebrations. It was a major operation with lots of flour, fruit, butter, milk and porter. We all waited patiently around the table until the cake was finished and placed in the oven. As soon as the oven door closed, my poor mother was besieged on all sides by requests to lick the wooden spoon, the whisk or even clean out the mixing bowl. The cake mix was very sweet and we weren't happy until we'd cleaned every last bit of it.

Writing my letter to Santa was another milestone before Christmas. It took days for me to think of the right things to ask from Santa. A number of drafts were written, torn up and written again before the final edition was deemed worthy to send. Once my brothers and sisters had their letters written, they were all placed in an envelope before being posted.

A week later, the postman delivered a letter addressed to "The Dwyer Children." I tore open the envelope and read the letter. It asked us to be good for our parents and be in bed early on Christmas Eve. To our amazement, it was signed Santa Claus. We were thrilled to have received an actual letter from the man himself. We never thought it strange that the reply used letterhead from Roche's Stores, a department store in Cork City. These letters proved that Santa was real and working for a big shop in the city. In our childish minds, Roche's Stores was the same as the North Pole. That night, I read the letter over and over, imaging Santa carefully wrapping my presents before departing for Beara. I dropped off to sleep with the letter folded carefully under my pillow.

It was a week away from Christmas Day and excitement was building. Maulin Mountain wore a white tablecloth of sleet as I joined my father and brothers in picking out a Christmas tree the following morning. We had a small grove of pines to the west of the house, and this usually yielded a good specimen. A chill wind whipped in from the west, causing me to draw my jacket over my face. We had a specific tree in mind as we searched. It had to be about six feet tall to be impressive but not so tall that it wouldn't fit in the room. It also had to have a nice conical shape.

We went from tree to tree, appraising each as a suitable candidate until we agreed on one with all of the right attributes. Once selected, my father cut the tree at its base with a saw and dragged it into the house. We placed it in a bucket of earth and gravel and stood back to admire it. I couldn't wait until that night to decorate it so I pestered my mother until she finally gave in and brought down the box of decorations from on top of her wardrobe. We wrapped the tree with red and blue tinsel until it glittered. We then carefully wound the lights around the tree before placing the slightly worn plastic star at the very top. We held our breath as I plugged in the lights and they flashed into life. No matter how many times we did this over the years, that moment always got a gasp of admiration from us all.

In the lead up to Christmas, the postman was busy delivering cards to our house and we waited excitedly for his arrival. I knew the usual time he passed the gate and listened out for the distinctive sound of his green van. I listened intently as he stopped at our neighbour's house and started up again, heading towards us. As he stopped outside our gate, there was a race to see who could get the post. That day, I had the thrill of accepting a bunch of letters of various sizes and colours. I walked towards the house, smiling broadly before handing over the mail to my parents with great ceremony. The ones we looked forward to the most were coloured bright red and had American stamps on them. Our aunts and uncles in the States sent impressive cards, often with a few dollars in them. Once they were read and admired, I added them to the others from home and abroad that were festooned on a string across the kitchen wall.

Christmas Eve was my favourite day of the year. The excitement of Santa's impending arrival was sky high, and there was still Christmas Day to come. Even though most children got their presents on Christmas Day, we got them on Christmas Eve night. From the moment my eyes fluttered open that morning, the countdown was on. The day was filled with the usual jobs but they were done with distraction. I got water from our spring well in the field below the house. I filled the red plastic bucket from the depths before returning with it. I then collected brisna for the fire in the morning. I brought along a piece of rope and when I had enough collected, I lay the brisna on the rope and tied it up in a bundle before swinging it onto my back. As I walked home, I was thrilled to see the light fading from the evening sun. The sticks were stored in an old room at the back of the house to keep them dry. Night fell and along with my brothers and sisters, we ate supper hurriedly. We had other things on our minds. My mother told me to light a few candles and place them on the windowsills, as it was traditional to do this. As I lit the last one, I glanced out to window to see if I could see any sign of Santa. The waiting game had begun.

I tried to distract myself by going to the Good Room to play some music. This was where guests were entertained and where we celebrated special occasions such as Christmas. A portrait of John F. Kennedy and his wife Jackie occupied a place of honour on the wall above the dining table. The floor was covered in carpet and the walls were plastered with wooden veneer. A heavy mahogany press at the end of the room contained my mother's best china. This room always smelled of furniture polish.

Between the fireplace and the armchair was a blue record player that my parents had brought from America. A floral decorated bag of records rested against the wall nearby. The Christmas tree twinkled in front of the window as I sat on the carpeted floor and thumbed through my parent's music collection. My favourite record was a single by Johnny Cash. It had "Forty Shades of Green" on one side and "Johnny Yuma" on the other. The records made a slight crackling sound when played. You could change the playing speed and make Johnny Cash sound like a chipmunk. I pulled out a vinyl disk in a cardboard sleeve called "Songs for the Season" and placed it on the player. A beautiful choral version of "Silent Night" filled the room. The open fire blazed behind me and the smell of the Christmas tree scented the air. "Not long more now," I thought.

When I became too restless to listen to music, I joined my brothers and sisters in the kitchen. They were watching a film on the television, but had their ears tuned to any strange noises outside that might indicate Santa's arrival. Our poor mother was demented with us running out the door at every sound when she was busy trying to get things ready for the Christmas dinner. She threatened us with the wooden spoon if we left the sitting room again. After a while, she returned to tell us that she thought she heard a van pulling off down the laneway. With that, we exploded from our seats and raced through the front door. Sure enough, at the corner of the house was a nest of cardboard boxes. "Santa came," went up the shrill cry of excitement as we claimed our prizes. We fought with each other over who opened what box, excitedly pulling out an assortment of toys. Within minutes, each of us was playing with our presents and showing off what Santa had brought us. Looking down the road, I thought I saw the lights of a van disappearing in the distance. I whispered my heartfelt thanks to Santa for giving me what I asked for.

My father came in later that evening after having been at the pubs in Eyeries Village. It was customary for the bars to give a free drink to regulars for Christmas so everyone availed of it. We excitedly showed him what Santa had brought us.

"Now, isn't Santa a great man all the same," he said, smiling. He produced a bottle of whiskey from the cupboard, and poured a drink for himself and a glass of sherry for my mother. "We didn't get all the toys that you got when I was young," he continued, reminiscing about the Christmases of his youth. "I got a wooden horse one Christmas and I had it for years. Another year, I received a tin whistle and an orange. Oranges were rare in those days," he said.

"Maybe Santa will bring you an orange next year if you're good," my mother joked, throwing her head back with laughter. Songs and stories continued long into the night.

We were up the next morning to go to Christmas Mass in Eyeries village. We were all tired from the late night but our mother made sure we were dressed in our best clothes. She ordered me to polish my shoes, which I did until I could see my vague reflection in them. When I was ready, I sat in the car and waited with my father. He combed his hair with Brylcreem, and its pleasant smell filled the car. We were the only ones ready and he didn't want to be late. He drummed his fingers on the steering wheel impatiently and hooted the horn a few times to hurry the others up. When we were all finally packed in, the car tore down the lane at speed. When we got to the village, the church was crammed with parishioners and many people stood at the back of the church. We squeezed into a pew alongside some neighbours. After mass, my parents chatted to friends and acquaintances that were home for Christmas while I joined my brothers and sisters around the crib at the top of the church.

Christmas dinner was the biggest feast of the year. My mother had spent the previous night getting everything ready. We sat around the dining table in the Good Room when my mother brought in the turkey on the china platter. The turkey was the centrepiece of the table. Brussels sprouts, carrots, roast and mashed potatoes were all served along with fizzy orange and lemonade. My father enjoyed a few bottles of Guinness while my mother took a glass of wine. Sherry trifle, jelly and cream were for dessert, and no one refused it even though we were nearly bursting.

The next day was St. Stephen's Day and everyone took it easy. However, it wasn't long before the first of the Wren-Boys came to the door. The Wren-Boys (pronounced Ran-Boys) were a tradition going back centuries. They wore facemasks, dressed up in old clothes and sang songs or played instruments at each house they called to, in exchange for some money. As I was old enough, I was allowed to go on the Wren if I took my brother Finbarr. We were both thrilled to be going. I salvaged a large tin can from the bin and cut a rectangular slot on the top to hold the rich fortune we were sure to collect. I put on a mask and an old jacket to disguise my appearance and Finbarr did the same. I took my tin whistle with me as I'd learned a few tunes in school.

We were both a bit nervous when we knocked on our first door, that of our neighbours. The poor people who answered it had to endure some terrible singing and tin whistle playing. However, they were kind and forgiving, putting coins in our collecting tin regardless. After that, our confidence grew with every door we knocked on. We even varied our act a bit and performed the well-known rendition of the St. Stephen's Day anthem.

The Wren, The Wren, The King of all birds,
St. Stephen's Day, he was caught in the furze,
Although he is little, his honour is great,

So rise up my fair lady and give us a treat.
Up with the kettle and down with the pots,
A schilling or two to bury the Wren.

By the end of the day, we had filled the tin many times over and our pockets were heavy with coins. We were delighted and excitedly discussed the comics and sweets we were going to buy. However, I also felt a tinge of sadness. It was the end of Christmas as far as I was concerned. There was no letters to write, no Santa to look forward to, no cake mix to enjoy. Even though Christmas had barely finished, I found myself looking forward to the next one again. Another long wait had begun.

A Christmas Childhood
by Patrick Kavanagh

One side of the potato-pits was white with frost —
How wonderful that was, how wonderful!
And when we put our ears to the paling-post
The music that came out was magical.

The light between the ricks of hay and straw
Was a hole in Heaven's gable. An apple tree
With its December-glinting fruit we saw —
O you, Eve, were the world that tempted me

To eat the knowledge that grew in clay
And death the germ within it! Now and then
I can remember something of the gay
Garden that was childhood's. Again

The tracks of cattle to a drinking-place,
A green stone lying sideways in a ditch
Or any common sight the transfigured face
Of a beauty that the world did not touch.

My father played the melodeon
Outside at our gate;
There were stars in the morning east
And they danced to his music.

Across the wild bogs his melodeon called
To Lennons and Callans.
As I pulled on my trousers in a hurry

I knew some strange thing had happened.

Outside the cow-house my mother
Made the music of milking;
The light of her stable-lamp was a star
And the frost of Bethlehem made it twinkle.

A water-hen screeched in the bog,
Mass-going feet
Crunched the wafer-ice on the pot-holes,
Somebody wistfully twisted the bellows wheel.

My child poet picked out the letters
On the grey stone,
In silver the wonder of a Christmas townland,
The winking glitter of a frosty dawn.

Cassiopeia was over
Cassidy's hanging hill,
I looked and three whin bushes rode across
The horizon — The Three Wise Kings.

An old man passing said:
'Can't he make it talk' —
The melodeon. I hid in the doorway
And tightened the belt of my box-pleated coat.

I nicked six nicks on the door-post
With my penknife's big blade —
There was a little one for cutting tobacco,
And I was six Christmases of age.

My father played the melodeon,
My mother milked the cows,
And I had a prayer like a white rose pinned
On the Virgin Mary's blouse.

10 KLONDIKE HOUSE

David stopped digging when he noticed something shiny sticking out of the brown earth. He picked it up and cleaned some of the caked soil from it.

"Look what I just found," he shouted. I stopped my digging and went over to see what my brother had discovered. Traces of muddy earth still clung to it but we could see that it was a letter opener with a decorated hilt and a broken handle. I took it from him and studied it, wondering how such a beautiful item had ended up in a muddy ditch near our house. We had been busy demolishing the ditch to make way for a new concrete wall when David made his discovery. I cleaned more earth from it with my sleeve and saw the detailed hilt more clearly. It showed figures of men swinging picks and hammers. Underneath this, there was an inscription.

When I read it aloud, we let out a collective whistle of amazement. It said, "Butte, Montana."

Growing up, Butte was as familiar to me as Cork or Dublin. Reminders of my family's connection to that city in Montana were dotted around my grandparent's house. A portrait of my great-grandfather Johnny "Báwn" Dwyer hung on a wall between pictures of the Irish patriots Wolfe Tone and Pádraig Pearse. The word báwn means white in Gaelic and was associated with our family due to them having blonde hair. Johnny's photograph was taken around 1914 while he was in Butte. The picture shows him resting his arm on a pedestal and wearing a fine suit of clothes. He sported a slender moustache and had a wry smile that suggested he was doing well, thank you very much.

In addition to the photograph, we had an old mining candleholder from Butte that my father kept in the shed. It was a sharp spike with a hook at the opposite end and. It had suffered from rust but its surface was smooth and it was still in good condition. The most visible reminder was an old black clock that sat on a shelf in the kitchen. It had also originated in Butte and had marked out the time for decades in the old house before it finally stopped working. Despite that, it retained its place of honour in the kitchen. All those things were reminders of the difficult and frightening journey that my ancestors had taken from that very house in search of a better life.

In the 1880s, economic conditions in Ireland were dire and especially so for rural farmers like my family. The scars of the Great Potato Famine thirty years earlier remained. Employment was scarce and most people eked out a living from the land, spending endless days of backbreaking toil in the fields. America was expanding at the time and thousands of people left Ireland for the promise of the New World. Among them were my great-granduncle Mike "Báwn" Dwyer and my great-grandfather Johnny "Báwn" Dwyer.

In 1882, copper had been discovered in Butte and a boom soon followed. People came from all over the world to work in the mines. Mike must have heard about the ready employment available there and left for Montana in 1888. He got a job in the mines and saved most of what he earned until he was able to send money home for his two sisters to join him in 1890.

Life in the mines must have been tough for Mike. It was gruelling work with very little rest. Many miners died in incidents such as rock falls, fires and premature explosions. Despite these dangers, the population of Butte swelled with immigrants. The people who arrived in Butte from our neighbouring parishes in Beara stuck together and tried to recreate the same sense of community and togetherness that they had enjoyed at home. From this sprang up Irish neighbourhoods with names like Hungry Hill (named after the highest mountain in Beara) and Corktown. It must have been a great comfort to Mike to have had so many friends and neighbours with him in Butte.

Even though he was doing well, Mike was looking for a way to break free of the arduous drudgery of mining. His chance arrived in 1897 when gold was discovered in the remote Klondike region of western Canada. A gold rush quickly ensued and Mike quit the mines to try his luck there. Just getting to the Klondike was a mammoth task. He caught a train to Seattle where he boarded a crowded boat to Skagway, the nearest port in Canada to the Klondike. At Skagway, the Canadian Mounted Police required every prospector to take a thousand pounds of food and at least the same weight in equipment, as the area they were headed to was wilderness and totally without supplies.

They also had to negotiate the formidable Chilkoot Pass, a two-thousand-foot climb with an incredibly steep incline. Mike would have had to make forty round trips over the pass to get all his food and equipment across. To make matters worse, 1897 was a record year for snow in the region. Parts of the Chilkoot Pass were buried in seventy feet of snow and avalanches killed many climbers on the way up. However, Mike made it across safely and then completed the final two-hundred-mile river journey to the Klondike on a barge. Along with thousands of other prospectors, he celebrated Christmas in 1897 in the tent city of Dawson on the banks of the Yukon River.

*Prospectors climbing
the Chilkoot Pass*

At that stage, most of the easily accessible gold was gone. The remaining deposits had to be extracted using old-fashioned mining, which Mike knew all too well. Within a year, most of the prospectors had left, disillusioned and poorer than when they arrived. Mike didn't find much gold but did stake a number of claims to some promising prospects. By 1900, mining companies had moved into the area and were buying up independent claims. Mike sold his claims and returned to Butte. He was one of the few to have done well from the gold rush, which made him comfortable but not rich. After he returned to Butte, he sent some money home to Ireland. It was used to build a new house in 1902, and it continues to be the family home to this day.

After his return, Mike wanted to start a business and so he bought into a saloon. It was a good choice as bars in Butte were open twenty-four hours a day, operating in three shifts to serve the waves of thirsty miners just after finishing their exhausting work. In 1909, the newly elected mayor of Butte named Mike as a police detective, despite Mike having no prior police experience. Mike was well known in Butte and took to the job with gusto. He sold his stake in the saloon to dedicate himself to his new role. He acquitted himself well and was promoted to lieutenant in 1911. Life was very rosy for Mike and he was about to be joined by another member of his family.

While Mike enjoyed success in America, Johnny "Báwn" Dwyer remained at home in Ireland to work on the farm. He married in 1898 and had five children, two of whom died in childhood. At that stage, his brothers and sisters had all departed to Butte, leaving him to manage the land with his elderly father. It must have been difficult for him to hear the success stories of his siblings in Butte while he toiled on the farm with little reward. In the end, the temptation of America proved too difficult to resist and in 1910, he left Ireland to join Mike in Butte. This meant leaving his family and the farm behind.

It would be easy to look back at his decision and be critical. However, they were very different times. It was common in those days for married men to leave their families and seek work abroad. Many went to England to work on farms for a season before returning home. Others left for America for many years, fully intending to return home once they had enough money saved for their families. Some returned, others didn't.

We don't know much about Johnny's activities but he spent a short time in Butte before he tried his luck in other mining towns in Montana and Utah. He returned home once to see his family in 1915. My grandfather, who would have been twelve at the time, recounted his visit years later.

"A man I did not recognise or remember showed up one day, and they told me that this was my father. The man stayed for a couple of weeks, and then went back to America. I never saw him again."

Johnny moved to Phoenix around 1917. From a letter to his parents around that time, it seems he was sick and he may have contracted the dreaded "miner's consumption". This was the greatest killer of miners, caused by the inhalation of quartz dust in the mines. People afflicted with this disease may have been told to move to a dry climate such as Phoenix to recuperate. This might explain why he ended up there. In any event, he didn't recover and died at the age of forty on November 22, 1918.

Mike enjoyed a successful career with the Butte Police Department until his retirement in 1923, when he opened a cigar shop across the road from his home. A few years later, he was diagnosed with cancer and underwent an operation at the Mayo Clinic in Rochester, Minnesota. While recovering, he contracted pneumonia and died in 1929.

Johnny "Báwn" Dwyer

Mike "Báwn" Dwyer at his police desk

When he was old enough, my grandfather Patrick took over the farm that his father Johnny had left behind. He married and had a family. Yet again, economic conditions in the 1950s and 1960s forced thousands of Irish to seek a better life abroad. My grandfather watched as one by one, his children immigrated to America. This time, they choose to settle in Boston instead of Butte. It was a repeat of what happened fifty years earlier. Only my father John returned from Boston to take over the farm. Unlike his grandfather Johnny, he stayed. Better still, he met my mother while in Boston and they were married shortly after they arrived home in Ireland.

* * *

Unlike my forebears, I was looking for excitement when I came to live in Boston. I wasn't there out of economic necessity and I already had a job secured with Fidelity Investments in the financial district. I found an apartment in Dorchester, the same area that my father had lived in years before.

On a visit to my Uncle Michael's house in Westwood one weekend, he told me about his search for the grave of Johnny "Báwn" Dwyer. He had located his final resting place in a cemetery in Phoenix. He passed me a Polaroid photograph of the headstone. He paid for a gravestone and for the ongoing upkeep of the plot. When I passed the photo back to him, he said, "You keep that. You might be visiting it at some stage." Over the Thanksgiving holiday that year, I decided to do just that.

My college friend Tadhg lived in Phoenix and I decided to visit him over the holiday weekend. Another friend Eoin, who lived in San Francisco at the time, joined us. We had a great weekend together as we chatted up girls in bars, visited the stunning Grand Canyon, and checked out the big Red Rocks in Sedona.

Despite those distractions, it was a grave I had really come to visit. Tadhg and Eoin joined me in searching for his final resting place. Before I left Boston, I had forgotten to ask my uncle Michael about the details of where to find the grave and the exact date of his death. All I knew for sure was that the grave was in Greenwood Cemetery on Van Buren Street. With the help of Tadhg and Eoin, we located the cemetery on a map and drove there. I expected to see a small graveyard like those in Ireland so I was shocked to see how big it was. Acres of headstones spread in all directions as we drove in. Trying to find a grave here with such little information would be daunting.

After parking, I went to the information office to see if they could help me with my search. I told the attendant that all I had was a name. He rubbed his chin ruefully and shook his head. It would take a long time to locate the grave with so little to go on, he admitted. Just when I was about to admit defeat, Eoin walked in and asked, "Was your great-grandfather called John Dwyer?" I nodded. "We found him," he said, beaming. I joined him outside and he pointed to the gravestone. I was gobsmacked. We had parked almost directly in front of it.

His grave looked cared for and a large palm tree shaded it from the blazing sun. What a foreign place this was compared to where he was born, I thought. How far from the familiar fields and misty hills of his birth he now lay. I noted from his headstone that it was just shy of the eightieth anniversary of his death. I said a silent prayer over his final resting place before leaving for the airport.

When I got back to Boston, I visited my uncle Michael in Westwood to tell him about my trip. I found him in his study, drawing up plans for a new construction project that he was working on. He listened intently to my story from Phoenix and shook his head in amazement.

"Isn't that something," he exclaimed, putting his hands behind his head and leaning back in his chair. "It's like he wanted you to find him."

On his desk were a scattering of papers, books, and that morning's opened mail. Alongside all this was a letter opener with a decorated hilt and a broken handle. I instantly recognised it as the one that we found years earlier as children. My uncle noticed my gaze and smiled.

"I use it to open my mail every morning," he beamed, picking up the letter opener and holding it like a piece of precious gold. "I'm guessing Johnny brought it back with him when he visited home," he said. "I've no idea how it could have ended up in the ditch but, here it is now."

Johnny and Mike paved the way for my family and countless others to settle in America. They, in turn, smoothed the way for my generation to work there. These immigrants sent money home to Ireland when times were hard, money that saved many families from outright poverty. Mike left his home in Beara and embarked on a journey that took him to the wilds of Canada in search of gold. If he hadn't gone there and sent some money back, the family home would never have been built. In his honour, my father erected a plaque outside the front gate of the house. The simple inscription read, "Klondike House."

On Irish American Shoulders
By Michael J. Dwyer

It's simple, it's complex, it's powerful
What analogy or metaphor will explain it?
To be Irish and American in Boston.
An unexplored, unexpressed state of being

Its uniqueness, its beauty, its depth
Its leadership, its compassion, its timelessness.
It is individual diversity seeking unity.
A cause for unity.

Something to love together.
It raises our sights. It moves us.
It is emotional.
It is as big as two cultures achieving what neither one can do
alone.

Its time has come.
I feel great hope.
Yours is a big American heart.
Familiarity.

Yes, I could make my home among you.
And I will learn your ways,
And I will sow in your land,
And you will help me reap.

And mine will be the silent shoulder,
Yours will be the sound,

Together we will strike a tune
Our renaissance has found.

Our children on our shoulders sit
The better to survey,
Their individual paths they find,
As we on backs surveyed.

FROM THE AUTHOR

Thanks for reading *Klondike House*, I hope you enjoyed it. Please feel free to visit my website and leave your comments as I'd love to hear from you.

www.JohnDwyerBooks.com
www.Facebook.com/JohnDwyerAuthor
www.Twitter.com/JohnDwyerBooks

John Dwyer

ALSO BY THE AUTHOR

High Road to Tibet: Travels in China, Tibet, Nepal and India. http://www.amazon.com/dp/B0045Y1PSI/

"You [John Dwyer] really do give an authentic feeling of the contrasting atmospheres as you move from place to place." - Dervla Murphy, international best-selling travel author.

"If you really want to find out about Asia, this book is a must buy for you." - Bibi Baskin, TV and radio presenter.

"It takes a very good travel book to make a Corkman want to leave his home - but one such book is *High Road To Tibet*" - Evening Echo

Made in the USA
Middletown, DE
13 August 2015